making math visual a

Grade 3
Multiplication and Division Games and Activities

created by
Colleen Uscianowski, PhD
edited by
Marshall Maa

 LUMINOUSLEARNING   www.luminouslearning.com

10 9 8 7 6 5 4 3 2 1

Published by Luminous Learning Inc, New York
Orders: www.luminouslearning.com
info@luminouslearning.com

ISBN 978-1-939763-24-2

Visit us online: **www.luminouslearning.com**

 facebook.com/LuminousLearning    twitter.com/luminouslearn

youtube.com/user/Luminouslearning    pinterest.com/luminouslearn

www.instagram.com/luminouslearning

LUMINOUSLEARNING

making math visual activity book
Grade 3 Multiplication and Division Games and Activities

Table of Contents

 LUMINOUSLEARNING   www.luminouslearning.com

HOW CHILDREN LEARN MULTIPLICATION AND DIVISION

Phases of multiplicative thinking

One way to think about students' development of multiplication facts is along a Concrete - Representational - Abstract continuum. Student progress through each of these three phases as they move from first learning the concept of multiplication and division until they eventually master their math facts.

Students in each of these phases need a different kind of instruction and practice in order to improve their multiplication and division skills. As you read about each phase below, consider which phase each student is in. Choose games and activities that target their current phase or help them advance to the next phase of multiplicative thinking.

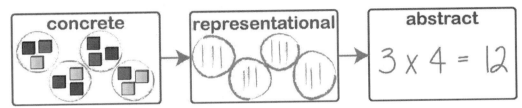

CONCRETE
In the beginning stages of learning to multiply, students need practice solving multiplication and division problems using concrete manipulatives such as counters and unifix cubes. Students in the concrete phase are gaining conceptual understanding and practicing their counting strategies.

REPRESENTATIONAL
After you spend time teaching multiplication problems using concrete materials, you can encourage students to use drawings or diagrams to solve multiplication problems. These drawings are similar to the manipulative in that they model the problem, but they are more abstract and therefore require more mathematical thinking.

Students in the representational phase are solidifying their conceptual understanding and counting strategies while beginning to apply more advanced reasoning skills to solve multiplication problems.

ABSTRACT
After students have practice first solving multiplication problems using concrete manipulatives and then drawings or diagrams, they will be ready to solve multiplication equations. This type of problem is abstract because it involves symbols that students need to interpret such as **x** and **÷**.

Students in the abstract phase have already gained a strong conceptual knowledge of multiplication. They are practicing their reasoning skills, which leads to fact mastery.

Counting Coins

5 times 5¢ equals 25 ¢

PLAYERS

2 - 4 students

MATERIALS

- 1 die per student
- Large collection of either nickel or dime manipulatives. You can use real nickels or dimes if you don't have the manipulatives, or use counters.
- Coin purse recording sheet (one per student) *Cut out and laminate these or put them in plastic sheet covers so that students can write on them with dry erase markers. You can choose to use the recording sheet that has the number line with students who struggle to count by 5s or 10s.

OBJECTIVE

Students roll the die to see how many coins they can put in their coin purse. You can choose to play with either nickels (skip counting by 5s) or dimes (skip counting by 10s). The student with the most money at the end of the game is the winner!

DIRECTIONS

1. Each student rolls one die. The number they roll is the number of nickels (or dimes) they need to place in their coin purse. For example, Student A rolls a 5 and places 5 nickels in their coin purse.
2. Students multiply to find the amount of money they have in their coin purse. For example, Student A has 5 nickels so student A multiplies: 5 nickels times 5¢ equals 25¢.
3. Each student fills in the blanks below the coin purse to show how much money they have
4. The student with the most amount of money wins that round and takes all the coins! If there is a tie, nobody wins that round and everybody keeps their own coins.
5. Start again from #1.
6. When there are no more coins left, students count up how much money they each have. The student with the most amount of money is the winner.

DIFFERENTIATION

- To make this activity easier, use a 6-sided die. To make this activity more challenging, use an 8-sided die.
- For those students who need more support, allow them to use the recording sheet that has the number line to help them skip count to find the total amount of money they have.
- Advanced students can play a challenge round using quarters.

Counting Coins

Recording Sheet - Nickels

 times 5¢ equals  ¢

Name: _____   Date: _____

Counting Coins

Recording Sheet - Nickels

[   ] times 5¢ equals [   ] ¢

Name: _____   Date: _____

Counting Coins

Recording Sheet - Dimes

times 10¢ equals  ¢

Name: _____   Date: _____

Counting Coins

Recording Sheet - Dimes

[ ] times 10¢ equals [ ] ¢

```
0   10   20   30   40   50   60   70   80   90
```

Dividing Dinos

PLAYERS

1 - 6 students

MATERIALS

- For each student, decide whether you want them to practice dividing by 2, 3, or 4. Each student will need the corresponding gameboard.
- Cut out or photocopy and assemble the corresponding spinner.
- Use counters as "dinosaur eggs."

DIRECTIONS

1. Tell students that the dinosaurs laid some eggs and want to organize their eggs into groups. Hand out a gameboard and spinner for each student. Each gameboard will help students to divide by 2, 3, or 4. Keep a collection of counters nearby.

2. Each student spins the spinner. When the spinner lands on a number, the student takes that many counters, or "dinosaur eggs." For example, if Student A landed on the number 12, they take 12 counters.

3. Each student needs to distribute their counters into the groups on the gameboard so that each group has the same number of counters. For example, if Student A has 12 counters and is dividing by 3, they will put 4 counters (or "dinosaur eggs") in each group.

4. Each student counts to find out how many dinosaur eggs they placed in each group. "I had 12 dinosaur eggs and divided them into 3 groups. I put 4 dinosaur eggs in each group."

5. Empty the gameboard and start again from #2!

DIFFERENTIATION

- Beginning students can practice dividing by 2 using the dividing by 2 gameboard and spinner.
- More advanced students can practice dividing by 3 or 4 using the dividing by 3 or 4 gameboard and spinner.
- You can challenge students by asking them to make a prediction before dividing their dinosaur eggs. "How many eggs do you think you'll put in each group? Let's divide your eggs and check to find out."

CAN YOU HELP THE DINOSAURS DIVIDE THEIR EGGS?
DIVIDE BY 2 SPINNER

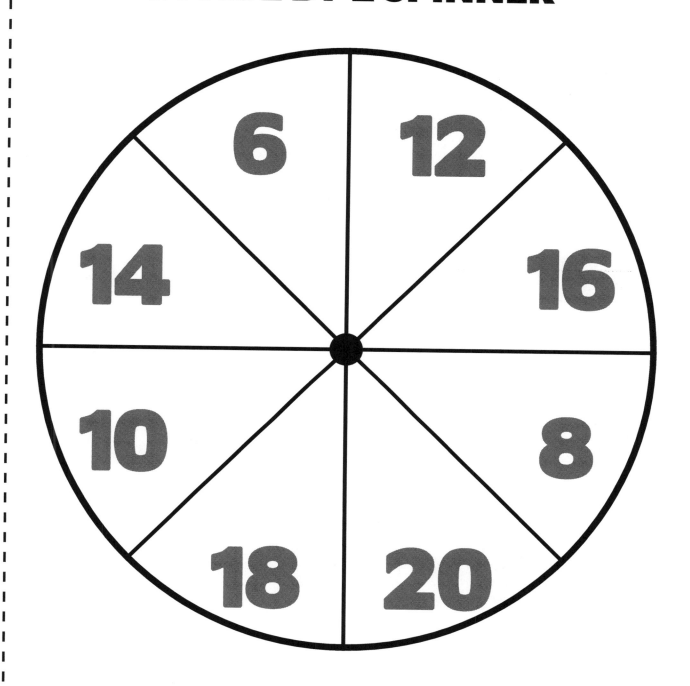

Directions for assembling the spinner:

1. Cut on the dotted line above to separate the spinner.

2. Cut out the arrow below.

3. Attach the arrow to the center of the spinner using a paper fastener.

CAN YOU HELP THE DINOSAURS DIVIDE THEIR EGGS?
DIVIDE BY 2 GAMEBOARD

CAN YOU HELP THE DINOSAURS DIVIDE THEIR EGGS?
DIVIDE BY 3 SPINNER

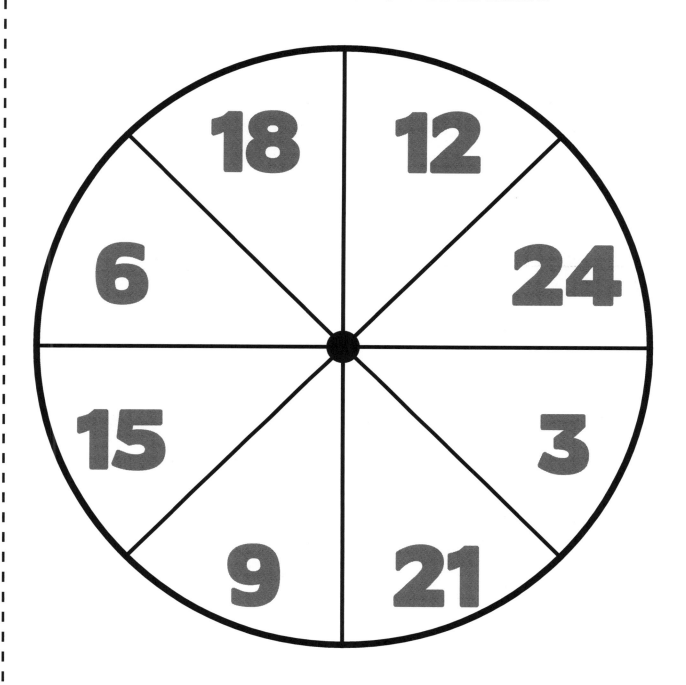

Directions for assembling the spinner:

1. Cut on the dotted line above to separate the spinner.
2. Cut out the arrow below.
3. Attach the arrow to the center of the spinner using a paper fastener.

CAN YOU HELP THE DINOSAURS DIVIDE THEIR EGGS?
DIVIDE BY 3 GAMEBOARD

CAN YOU HELP THE DINOSAURS DIVIDE THEIR EGGS?
DIVIDE BY 4 SPINNER

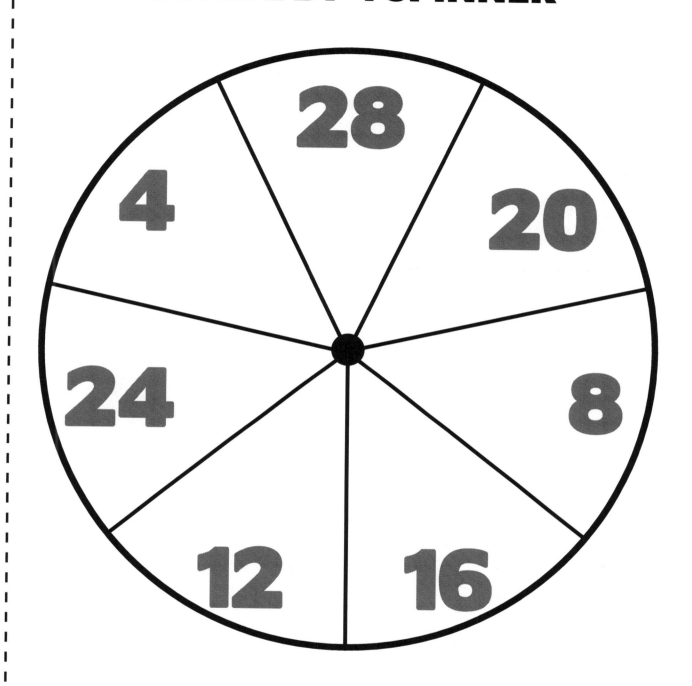

Directions for assembling the spinner:

1. Cut on the dotted line above to separate the spinner.

2. Cut out the arrow below.

3. Attach the arrow to the center of the spinner using a paper fastener.

CAN YOU HELP THE DINOSAURS DIVIDE THEIR EGGS?
DIVIDE BY 4 GAMEBOARD

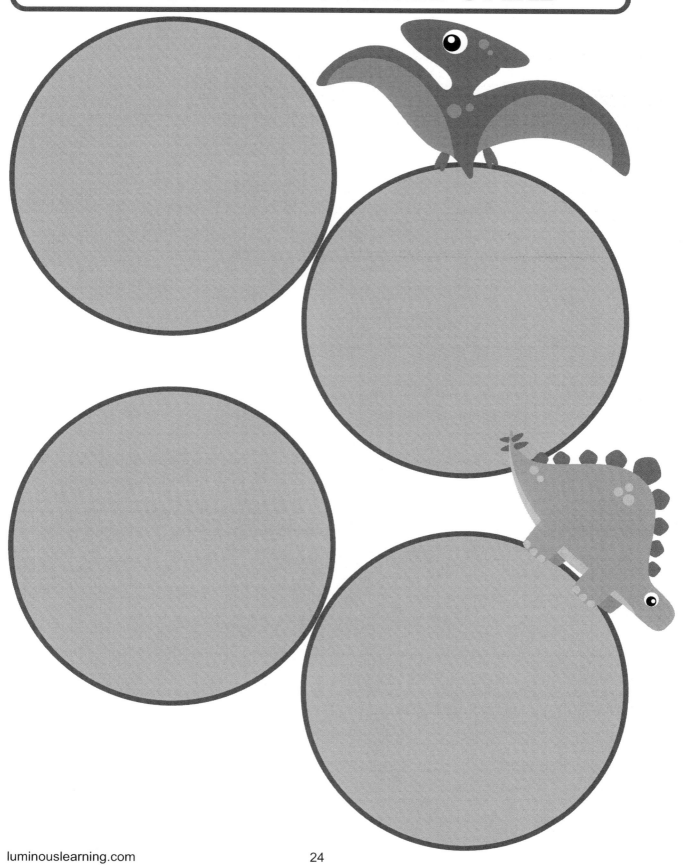

Ready Set Go!

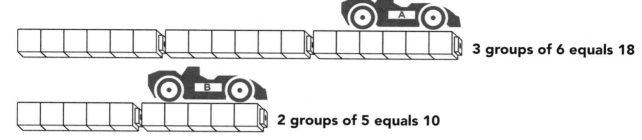

3 groups of 6 equals 18

2 groups of 5 equals 10

PLAYERS

2 - 4 students

MATERIALS

- 2 dice per student
- Linking cubes such as unifix cubes. Use counters if you don't have connecting cubes
- *Ready Set Go!* recording sheet (photocopy to make one printout per student)

OBJECTIVE

Students are driving race cars. The dice tells them how many yards their race car travels towards the finish line. The student whose race car travels the farthest wins that round!

DIRECTIONS

1. Each student rolls 2 dice. The first number they roll tells them how many groups of unifix cubes they should make. The second number they roll tells them how many unifix cubes they should put in each group. For example, Student A rolls a 3 and a 6. They need to make 3 groups with 6 unifix cubes in each group.
2. Students fill in their recording sheet to indicate the number of groups, the number of unifix cubes, and the total. For example, Student A should write, "3 groups of 6 equals 18."
3. Each student links their groups of unifix cubes together. They line up their stacks of unifix cubes. Each stack represents the distance their racing car has traveled towards the finish line. The student whose stack of unifix cubes is the longest has traveled the furthest distance towards the finish line.
4. Students start over from #2 and continue playing!

DIFFERENTIATION

- Use 6-sided dice with beginning students and 8-sided dice with advanced students.
- To challenge students, have them keep track of the product each time they roll the dice. At the end of the game, students add up their products. The student with the largest sum has the racing car that traveled the farthest distance and wins the game!

Name: _____   Date: _____

 groups of equals

 groups of equals

 groups of equals

 groups of equals

 groups of equals

 groups of equals

28

Multiplying Money

PLAYERS

1 - 6 students

MATERIALS

- Small paper plates
- 2 dice (6-sided or 8-sided)
- Penny manipulatives (You can use real pennies or counters if you don't have pretend pennies)
- Photocopy or cut out of the recording sheet on the next page (one per student)

4 groups of 6 pennies is 24 pennies in all

DIRECTIONS

1. Each student rolls both dice. Students write the first number in the first blank as the number of groups on their recording sheet. Students write the second number in the second blank as the number of pennies. For example, if a student rolls a 4 and a 6, they should write: _4_ groups of _6_ pennies.

2. Students take the number paper plates that corresponds to the first number they rolled. In the example above, the student rolled a 4 first. The student should take 4 paper plates to make 4 groups.

3. Students take the number of pennies that corresponds to the second number they rolled. In the example above, the student rolled a 6. The student should place 6 pennies on each plate.

4. Students count the total number of pennies on all the plates to find the product. They fill in the product on their recording sheet: _4_ groups of _6_ pennies is _24_ pennies in all.

5. Students clear their plates and start again from #1!

DIFFERENTIATION

- More advanced students can work independently on this activity while students who need more support can work in pairs.
- To make this activity easier, use two 6-sided dice. To make this activity more challenging, use one 6-sided and one 8-sided dice. To make this activity even more challenging, use two 8-sided dice.
- If students are successfully counting all the pennies to find the product, encourage them to use another strategy, such as skip counting.

Name: _____ Date: _____

Multiplying Money

Recording Sheet

 groups of pennies is  pennies in all

 groups of pennies is pennies in all

 groups of pennies is pennies in all

 groups of pennies is pennies in all

groups of pennies is pennies in all

 groups of pennies is pennies in all

Array City

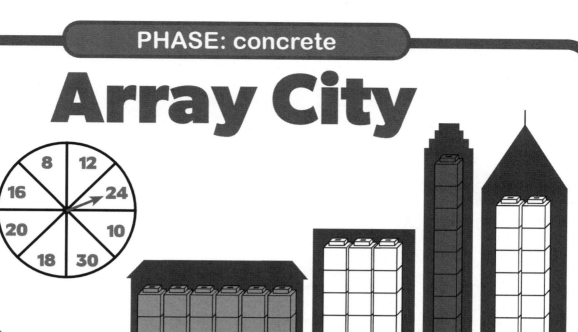

PLAYERS

1 - 4 students

MATERIALS

- Linking cubes such as unifix cubes. You can use square counters (such as foam tiles) if you don't have unifix cubes.
- Cut out or photocopy and assemble the spinner. You can use either the spinner with smaller or larger numbers, depending on the skill level of your students.
- Optional: Large sheet of paper, such as chart paper

OBJECTIVE

Students arrange the linking cubes into even stacks. These stacks represent buildings. Students can put these buildings together to create a city of arrays.

DIRECTIONS

1. Each student spins the spinner. The number they land on tells them how many linking cubes to take.
2. Students arrange the linking cubes into stacks, with the same number of cubes in each stack. For example, Student A lands on 24 and takes 24 linking cubes. Student A can create 6 stacks with 4 cubes in each stack, or 1 stack with 24 cubes, or 12 stacks with 2 cubes in each stack, etc.
3. As students continue to spin the spinner and create buildings with arrays, they can place their buildings together on a large sheet of paper to create a city of arrays. When students are done making arrays, they can draw buildings around the arrays on the chart paper.

DIFFERENTIATION

- Use the spinner with smaller numbers with beginning students.
- Use the spinner with larger numbers with advanced students.

ARRAY CITY SPINNER

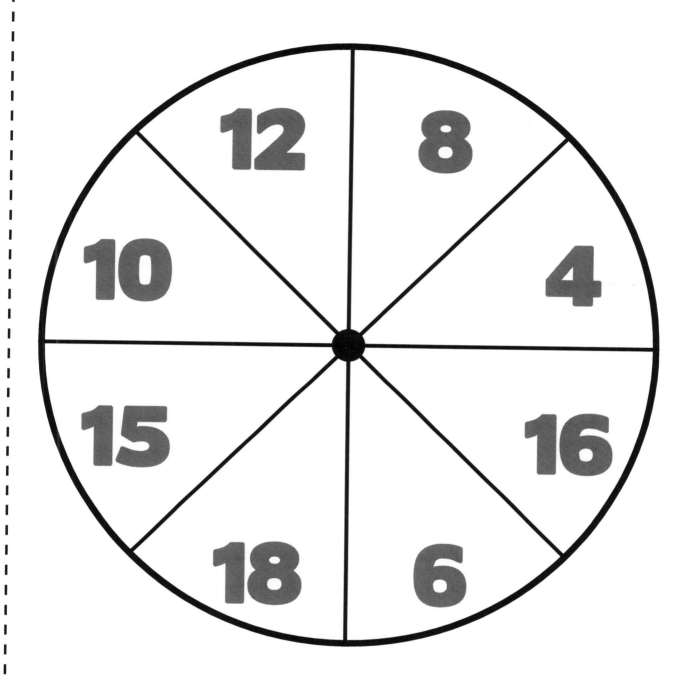

Directions for assembling the spinner:

1. Cut on the dotted line above to separate the spinner.
2. Cut out the arrow below.
3. Attach the arrow to the center of the spinner using a paper fastener.

ARRAY CITY SPINNER

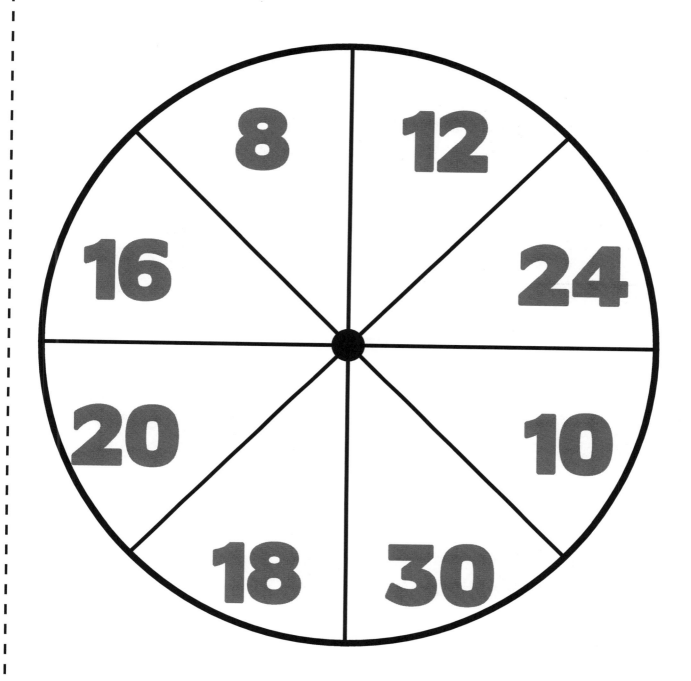

Directions for assembling the spinner:

1. Cut on the dotted line above to separate the spinner.

2. Cut out the arrow below.

3. Attach the arrow to the center of the spinner using a paper fastener.

Buggin' Out

3 groups of
5 equals 15

PLAYERS

2 - 4 students

MATERIALS

- Buggin' Out gameboard. Cut out or photocopy on thick card stock. Tape or glue both sides of the gameboard together.
- One set of Buggin' Out cards. Cut out each card.
- Counters or game pieces
- Die

OBJECTIVE

Students take turns answering the multiplication problem represented by groups on each card. Then they roll the die to see how many spaces to move around the gameboard. The first player to reach the finish line wins

DIRECTIONS

1. Shuffle the buggin' out cards and place face-down in a pile. Have students place their game pieces on START.
2. Students roll the die to see who goes first. The student who rolls the highest number goes first and they continue to take turns in a clockwise direction.
3. The first student turns over the top card in the deck. The student looks at the number of groups and the number of squares in each group to figure out the product. For example, Student A turns over a card that shows 3 groups with 5 squares in each group. Student A says: "3 groups of 5 equals 15."
4. The student rolls the die and moves their game piece according to the number they rolled. For example, if Student A rolls a 4, they will move their game piece ahead 4 squares.
5. The next student takes a turn and turns over the next card in the deck. Students continue to take turns solving the multiplication equations on each card and rolling to die to move their game pieces ahead. The first student to reach FINISH wins!

DIFFERENTIATION

- If students need more support, you can write down the number of groups and squares in each group on each Buggin' Out card.
- Students who need more support can partner up and play as a team. Students who need less support can play individually.

START

Move ahead 2 spaces

Take an extra turn

Lose a turn

Move
ahead 3
spaces

Lose
a turn

Move
back 3
spaces

FINISH

Move
back 2
spaces

Buggin' Out Cards

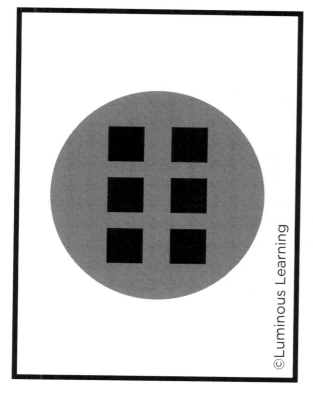

©Luminous Learning

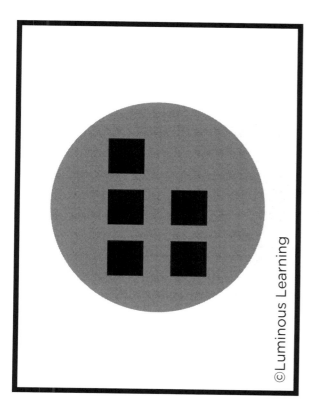

©Luminous Learning

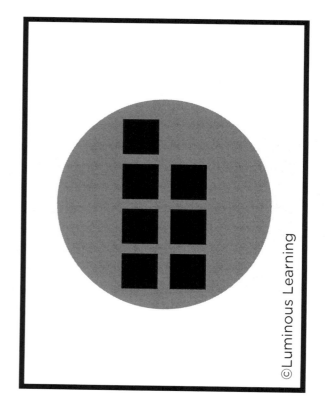

©Luminous Learning

©Luminous Learning

Buggin' Out Cards

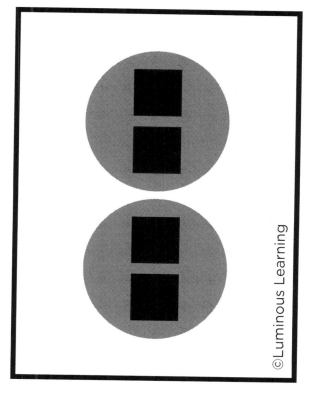

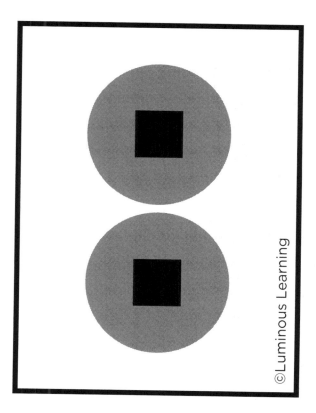

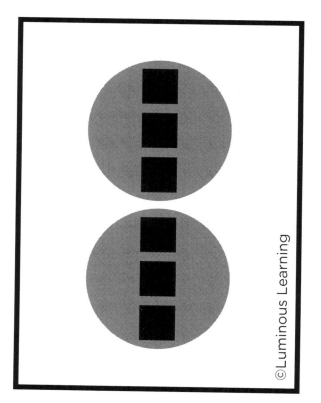

Buggin' Out Cards

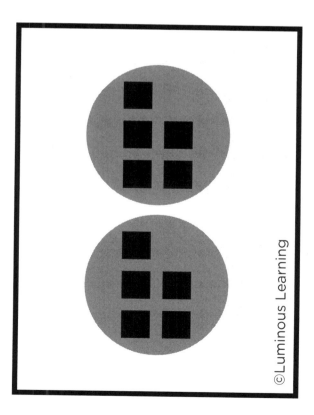

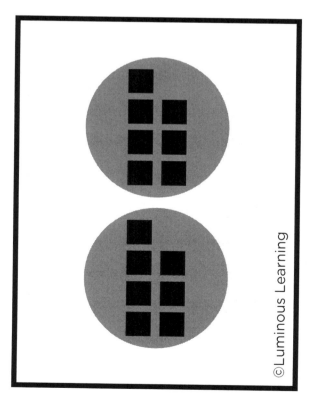

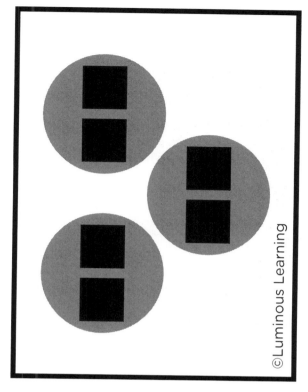

©Luminous Learning

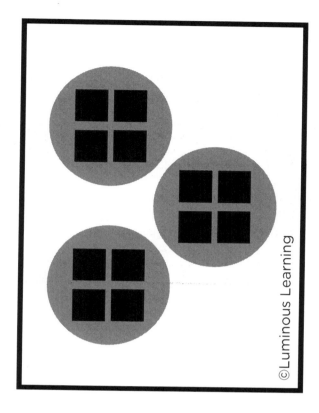

©Luminous Learning

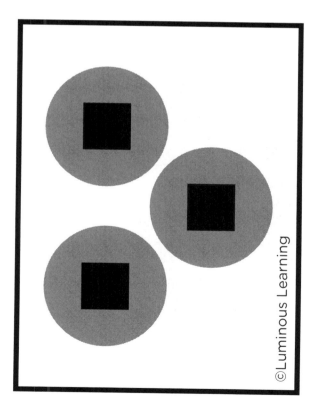

©Luminous Learning

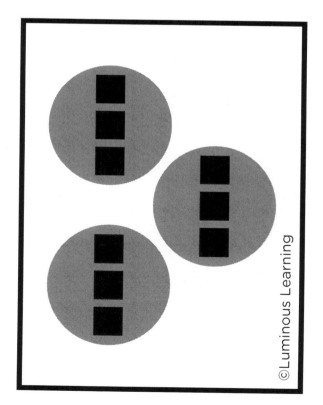

©Luminous Learning

Buggin' Out Cards

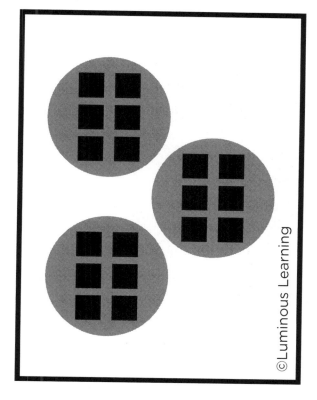

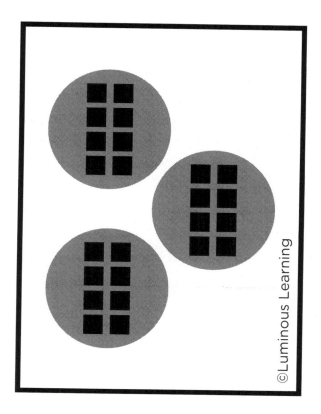

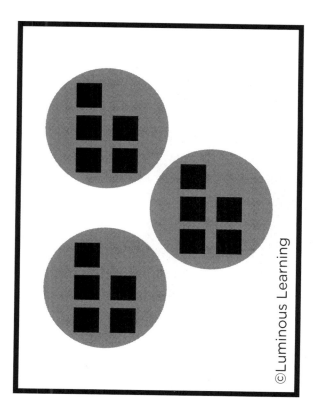

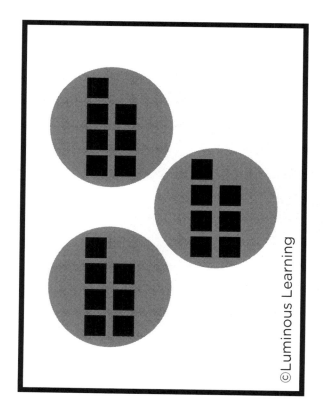

©Luminous Learning

Buggin' Out Cards

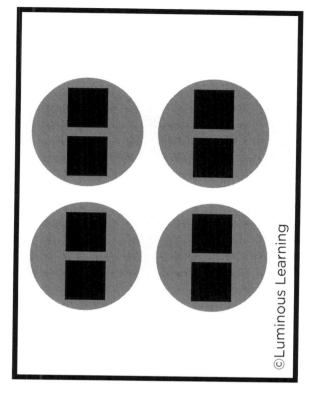

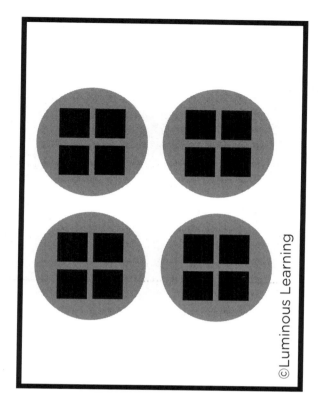

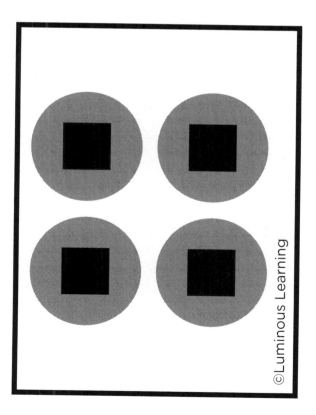

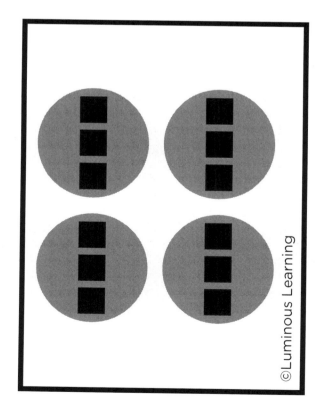

Buggin' Out Cards

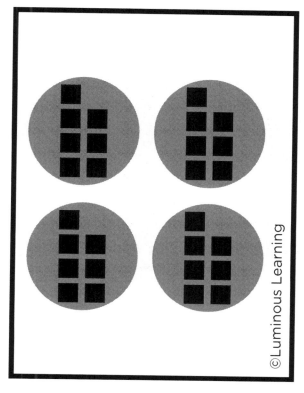

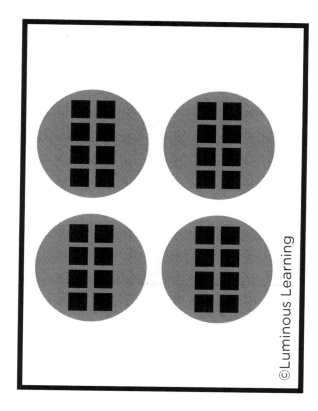

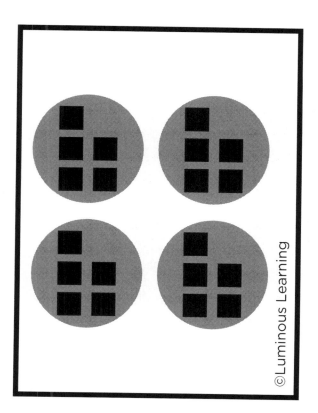

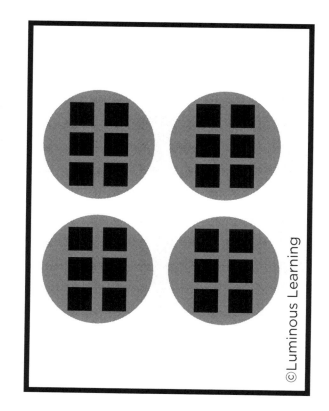

Buggin' Out Cards

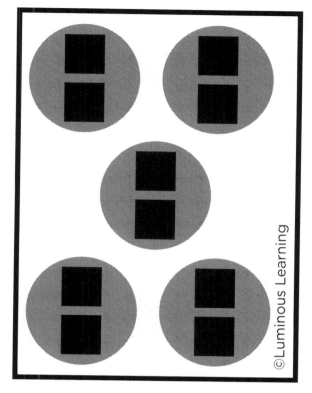

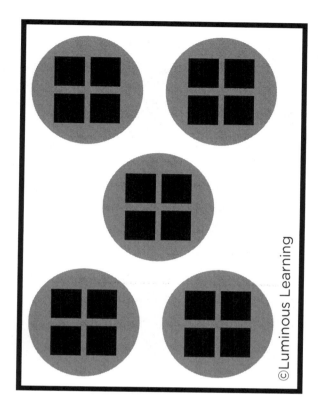

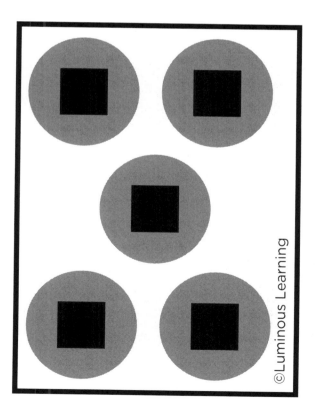

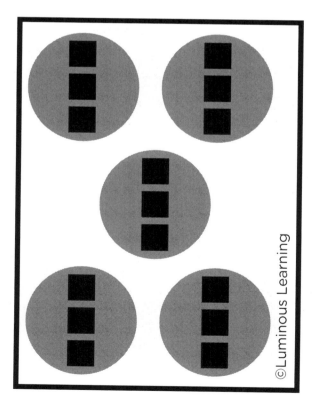

Buggin' Out Cards

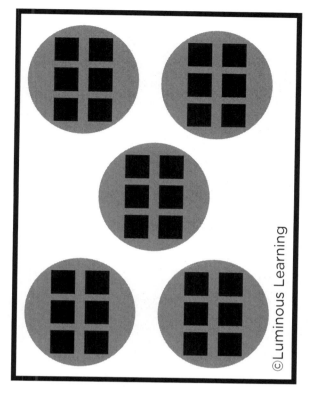

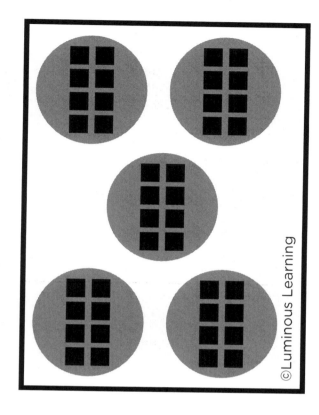

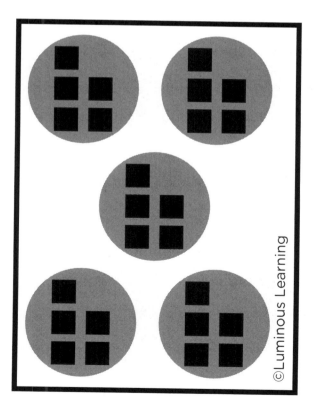

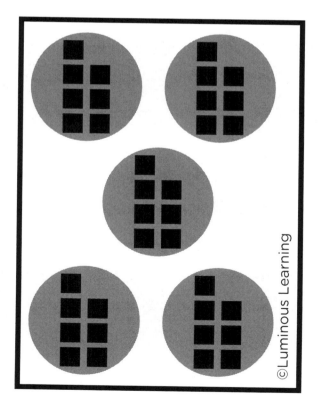

Garden Arrays

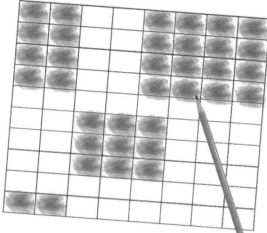

PLAYERS

2 students

MATERIALS

- 2 dice (6-sided or 8-sided)
- Pencil, marker, or crayon
- Cut out of the grid paper (one per game). The easier grid paper is on pg. 66 and the more challenging grid paper is on pg. 68.

OBJECTIVE

Students take turns planting arrays of flowers in the garden. The last student who can successfully plant flowers by shading in squares on the grid is the winner.

DIRECTIONS

1. Tell students that they are planting flowers in the garden. Each array they shade in represents one group of flowers that they are planting.

2. Student 1 starts. Student 1 rolls both dice. The two numbers become a multiplication equation that the student needs to shade in anywhere on the grid paper, thereby creating an array. For example, if the student rolls a 3 and a 2, they need to shade in 3 rows and 2 columns or 2 rows and 3 columns.

3. Each student needs to read their equation aloud after they shade in the squares. For example, after shading in 3 rows and 2 columns, student 1 says: "3 times 2 equals 6."

4. Now it's the next student's turn. Student 2 rolls both dice. Student 2 shades in the correct number of rows and columns anywhere on the board to create an array that represents the multiplication equation they rolled with the dice.

5. Students continue to take turns rolling the dice and shading in squares on the grid that represent the multiplication equation. The objective of the game is to be the last player who can take a turn and "plant flowers in the garden." Once a student rolls the dice but has nowhere left on the grid paper to shade in squares, the other player is the winner!

DIFFERENTIATION

- To make this activity easier, use 6-sided dice and the grid paper on page 66.
- To make this activity more challenging, use 8-sided dice and the grid paper on page 68.
- If students are successfully counting all the squares to find the product, encourage them to use another strategy, such as skip counting or relying on a known fact.

Name: _____   Date: _____

Garden Arrays

Name: _____   Date: _____

Garden Arrays

Doubling Hat

PLAYERS

1 - 4 students

MATERIALS

- Doubling Hat cards. Cut out each individual card and distribute one set of cards per student. You can laminate the cards so that students can write on them with dry erase markers.
- A dark-colored pencil, colored pencil, crayon, or dry erase marker.
- Optional: Counters, for those students who need more support.

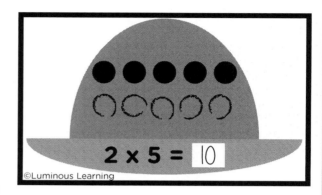

2 x 5 = 10

©Luminous Learning

OBJECTIVE

This is a magical doubling hat! Everything that goes into the hat doubles and you take out twice as many. Students double the number on each card and fill in the multiplication equation.

DIRECTIONS

1. Shuffle the doubling hat cards and distribute one set of cards to each student.
2. Students draw the top card in their deck.
3. They count the number of dots on the card. Then students draw to show the doubled number of dots. For example, Student A counts 5 dots on their card. Student A draws 5 more dots on the card to show that 5 is doubled when it goes into the doubling hat.
4. Students fill in the multiplication equation on the card. For example, Student A finishes the equation: 2 x 5 = 10.
5. After finishing one card, students take the next card in their deck and start again from #3.

DIFFERENTIATION

- You can use counters with those students who need more support. Students can model the multiplication equation by making groups with the counters.
- To make the activity more concrete, you can have students pretend that the dots are something concrete that they would want to double, such as pennies, cookies, crackers, toys, etc. Students can imagine that when they put 5 cookies into the doubling hat, for example, they take out 10 cookies.

Doubling Hat Cards

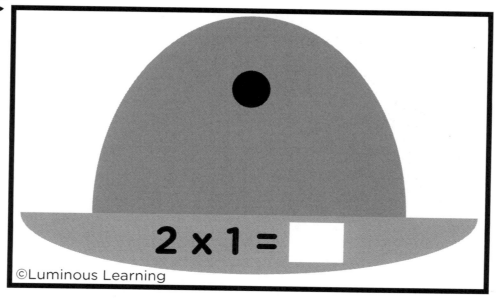

2 x 1 =

©Luminous Learning

2 x 2 =

©Luminous Learning

2 x 3 =

©Luminous Learning

Doubling Hat Cards

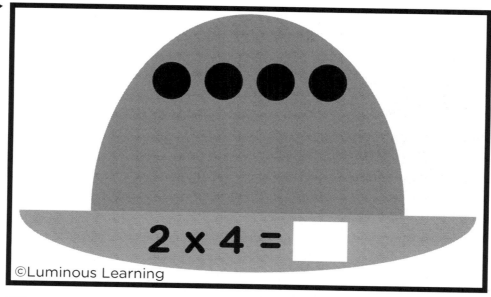

2 x 4 =

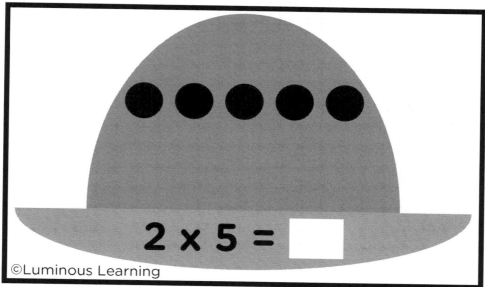

2 x 5 =

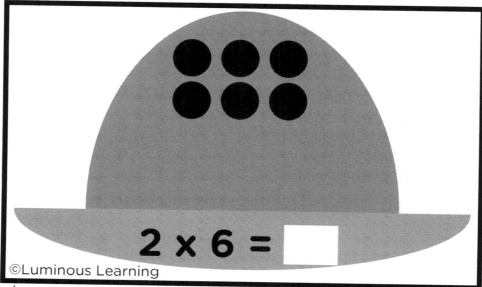

2 x 6 =

Doubling Hat Cards

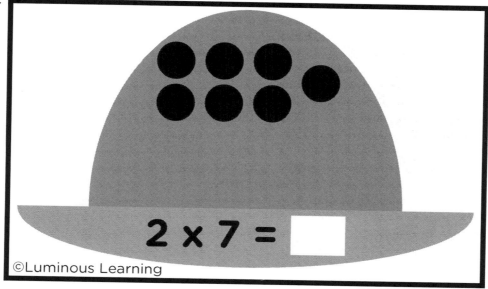

2 x 7 =

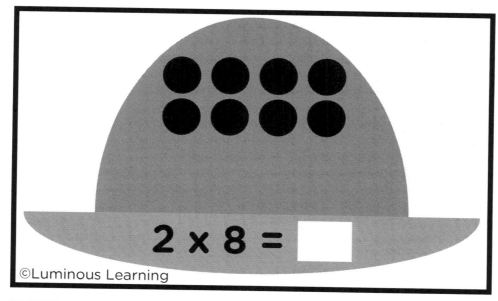

2 x 8 =

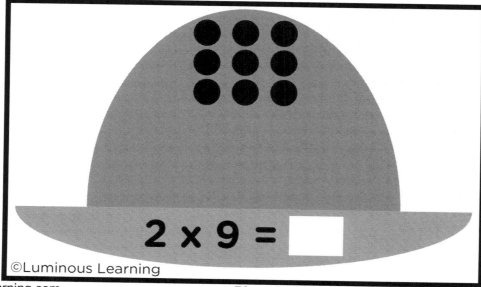

2 x 9 =

Railroad Division

$$8 \div 2 = \boxed{4}$$

railroad   cars per   groups
cars   groups

PLAYERS

1 - 6 students

MATERIALS

- Railroad division cards. Cut out each card. You can laminate the cards so that students can write on them with dry erase markers.
- Pencils or dry erase markers.
- Optional: Counters for those students who need extra support.

OBJECTIVE

Students own a railroad company! They are manufacturing new railroad cars and need to decide how to group the railroad cars together.

DIRECTIONS

1. Shuffle the railroad division cards and distribute cards to each student. You can decide how many cards to give each student.
2. Students read the division equation. For example, Student A reads, "8 railroad cars divided by 2 cars per group makes how many groups?"
3. Students can use the visual rectangles and the number line to help them divide. For example, Student A can circle groups of 2 cars then count how many groups they made: "1, 2, 3, 4 groups. 8 railroad cars divided by 2 cars per group makes 4 groups."
4. After finishing one card, students take another card and start again from #2.

DIFFERENTIATION

- Use the cards with smaller numbers with beginner students.
- Use the cards with larger numbers with more advanced students.
- You can use unifix cubes or counters with those students who need more support. Model the division problem using these physical manipulatives.
- Students may confuse "cars per group" with "groups." Be prepared to model the difference between counting the groups and the units per group.

Railroad Division

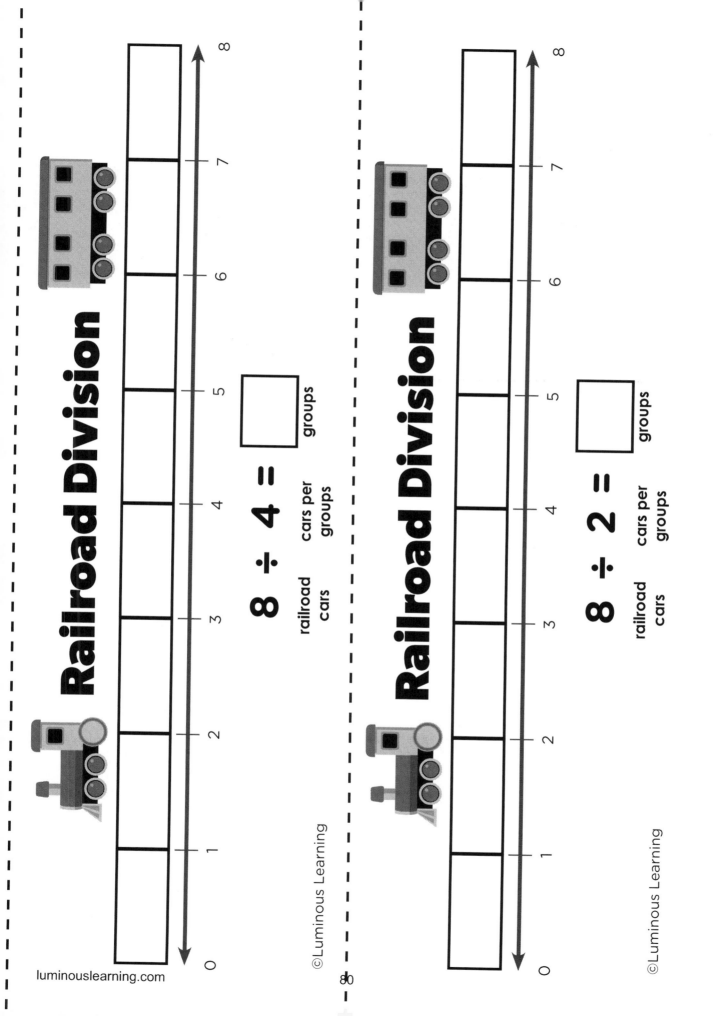

$8 \div 4 =$

railroad cars

cars per groups

groups

luminouslearning.com

©Luminous Learning

80

Railroad Division

$8 \div 2 =$

railroad cars

cars per groups

groups

©Luminous Learning

Railroad Division

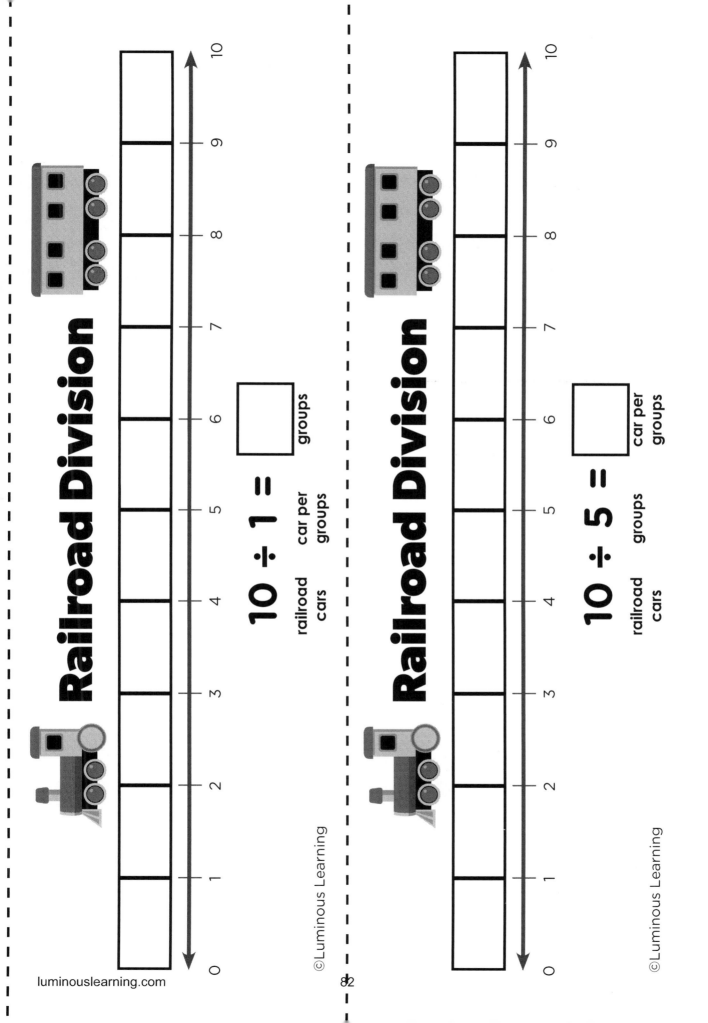

0 1 2 3 4 5 6 7 8 9 10

10 ÷ 1 =

railroad   car per
cars   groups

☐ groups

Railroad Division

0 1 2 3 4 5 6 7 8 9 10

10 ÷ 5 =

railroad   groups
cars

☐ car per
   groups

Railroad Division

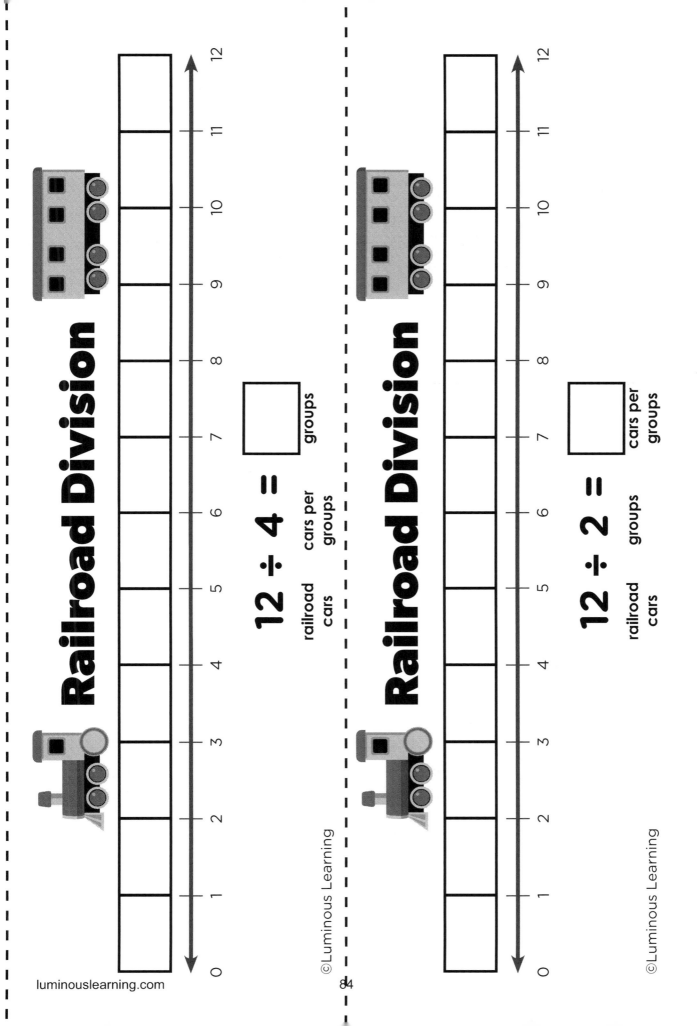

0 1 2 3 4 5 6 7 8 9 10 11 12

12 ÷ 4 =

railroad
cars

□ cars per
groups

groups

luminouslearning.com

©Luminous Learning

Railroad Division

0 1 2 3 4 5 6 7 8 9 10 11 12

12 ÷ 2 =

railroad
cars

groups

□ cars per
groups

84

©Luminous Learning

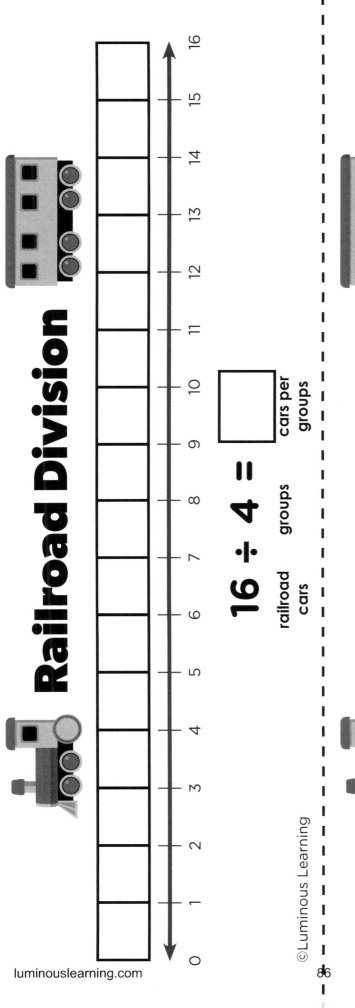

Railroad Division

luminouslearning.com

$16 \div 4 =$

$\Box$ cars per groups

railroad cars | groups

0 1 2 3 4 5 6 7 8 9 10 11 12 13 14 15 16

©Luminous Learning

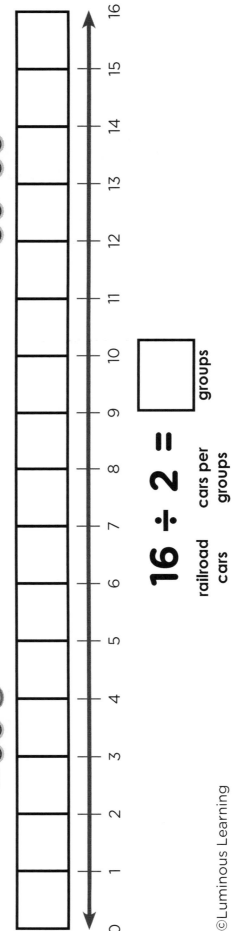

Railroad Division

$16 \div 2 =$

$\Box$ groups

railroad cars | cars per groups

0 1 2 3 4 5 6 7 8 9 10 11 12 13 14 15 16

86

©Luminous Learning

Railroad Division

$$16 \div 16 =$$

railroad
cars

groups

[ ] cars per
groups

0 1 2 3 4 5 6 7 8 9 10 11 12 13 14 15 16

Railroad Division

$$16 \div 8 =$$

railroad
cars

cars per
groups

[ ] groups

0 1 2 3 4 5 6 7 8 9 10 11 12 13 14 15 16

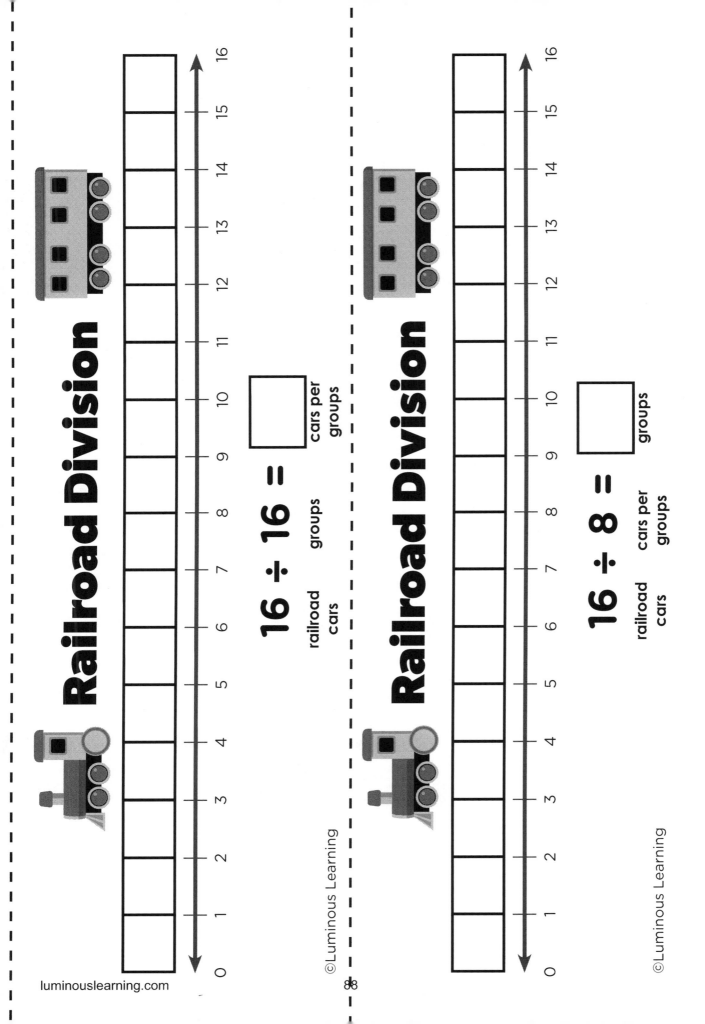

Railroad Division

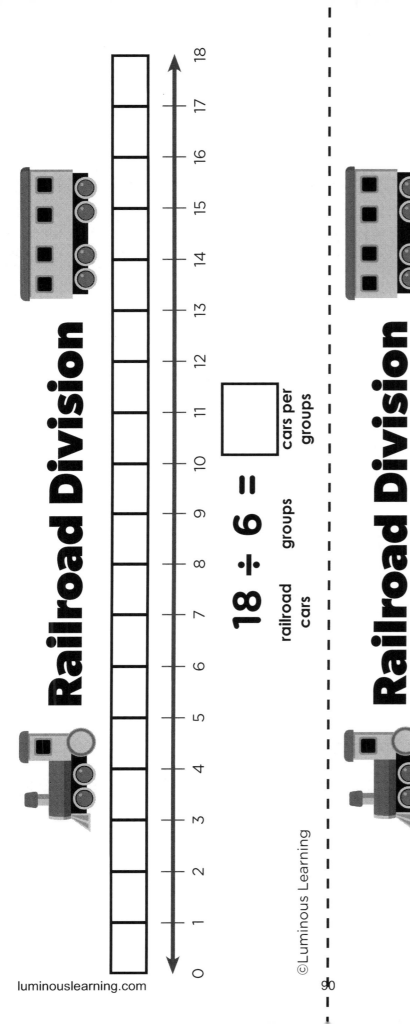

$18 \div 6 =$

___ groups

railroad cars

[ ] cars per groups

Railroad Division

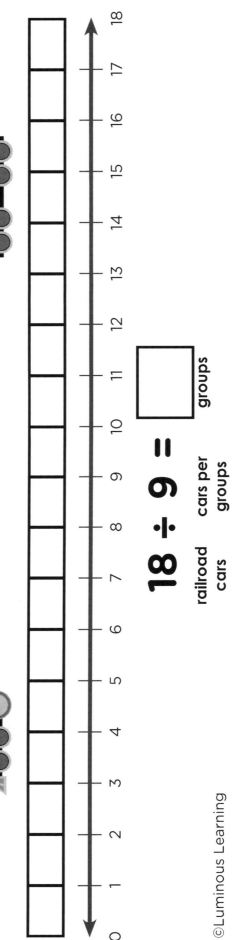

$18 \div 9 =$

cars per groups

railroad cars

[ ] groups

Railroad Division

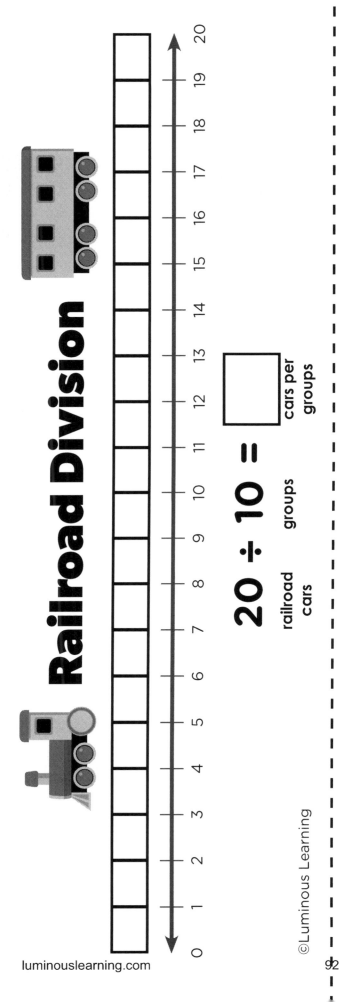

0 1 2 3 4 5 6 7 8 9 10 11 12 13 14 15 16 17 18 19 20

20 ÷ 10 =

railroad cars ÷ groups = □ cars per groups

Railroad Division

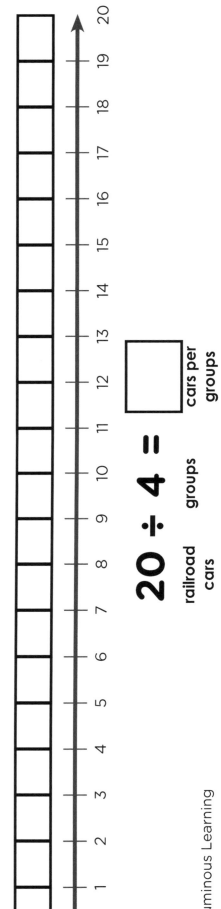

0 1 2 3 4 5 6 7 8 9 10 11 12 13 14 15 16 17 18 19 20

20 ÷ 4 =

railroad cars ÷ groups = □ cars per groups

Railroad Division

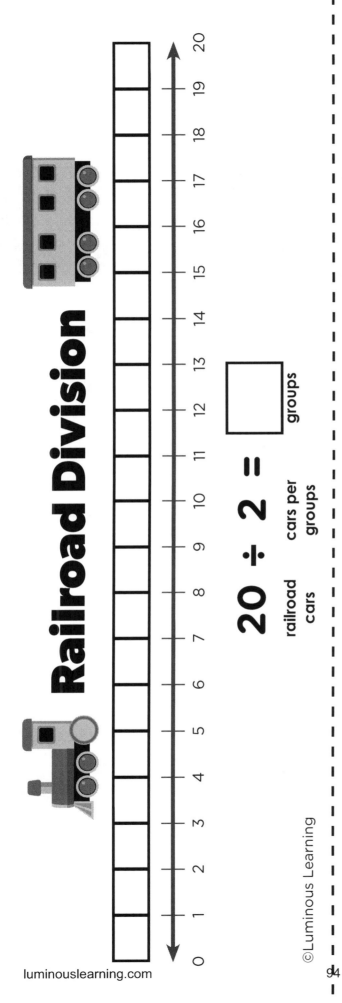

20 ÷ 2 =

railroad
cars

cars per
groups

[ ] groups

0 1 2 3 4 5 6 7 8 9 10 11 12 13 14 15 16 17 18 19 20

Railroad Division

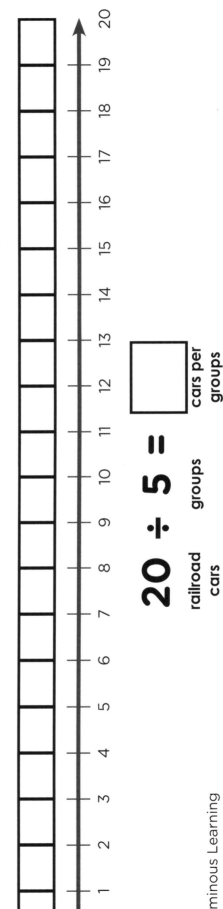

20 ÷ 5 =

railroad
cars

groups

cars per
groups

[ ]

0 1 2 3 4 5 6 7 8 9 10 11 12 13 14 15 16 17 18 19 20

Railroad Division

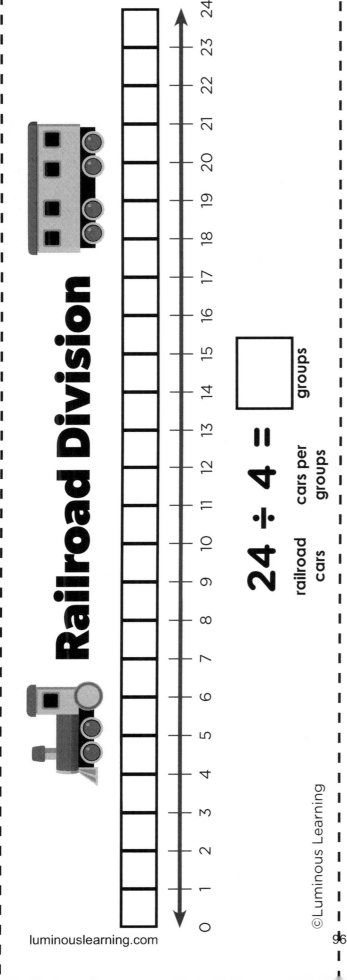

$24 \div 4 =$

railroad cars

___ cars per groups

___ groups

Railroad Division

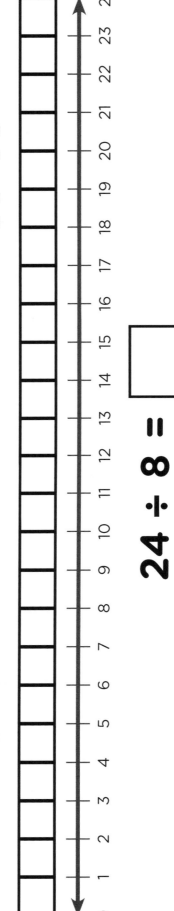

$24 \div 8 =$

railroad cars

___ cars per groups

___ groups

Railroad Division

 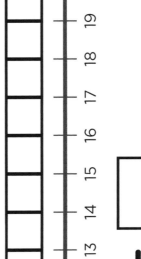

0 1 2 3 4 5 6 7 8 9 10 11 12 13 14 15 16 17 18 19 20 21 22 23 24

24 ÷ 3 =

railroad
cars

groups

cars per
groups

Railroad Division

0 1 2 3 4 5 6 7 8 9 10 11 12 13 14 15 16 17 18 19 20 21 22 23 24

24 ÷ 2 =

railroad
cars

groups

cars per
groups

Railroad Division

0 1 2 3 4 5 6 7 8 9 10 11 12 13 14 15 16 17 18 19 20 21 22 23 24 25 26 27 28

28 ÷ 4 =

□

railroad   groups
cars

cars per
groups

Railroad Division

0 1 2 3 4 5 6 7 8 9 10 11 12 13 14 15 16 17 18 19 20 21 22 23 24 25 26 27 28

28 ÷ 7 =

□

railroad   groups
cars

cars per
groups

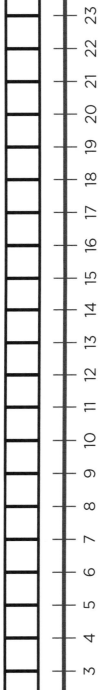

Railroad Division

0 1 2 3 4 5 6 7 8 9 10 11 12 13 14 15 16 17 18 19 20 21 22 23 24 25 26 27 28 29 30

30 ÷ 3 =

railroad cars

groups

☐ cars per groups

Railroad Division

0 1 2 3 4 5 6 7 8 9 10 11 12 13 14 15 16 17 18 19 20 21 22 23 24 25 26 27 28 29 30

30 ÷ 5 =

railroad cars

groups

☐ cars per groups

Railroad Division

$$30 \div 15 =$$

railroad cars	cars per groups
	groups

0 1 2 3 4 5 6 7 8 9 10 11 12 13 14 15 16 17 18 19 20 21 22 23 24 25 26 27 28 29 30

Railroad Division

$$30 \div 6 =$$

railroad cars	cars per groups
	groups

0 1 2 3 4 5 6 7 8 9 10 11 12 13 14 15 16 17 18 19 20 21 22 23 24 25 26 27 28 29 30

Multiplying Monsters

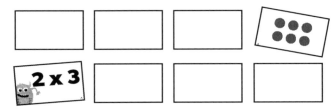

PLAYERS

1 - 4 students

MATERIALS

- *Multiplying Monsters* cards. There are two sets of cards: set A and set B. Each set has 12 cards with multiplication problems and 12 cards with arrays. Set A has simpler problems and set B has harder problems. You can use either set or combine sets, depending on the needs of your students. After choosing a set, cut out all of the cards. Alternatively, you can photocopy the cards on thick card stock so that students cannot see through the cards.

OBJECTIVE

To collect the most cards by the end of the game.

DIRECTIONS

1. Shuffle the *Multiplying Monsters* cards. Turn over each card so that they are facing down and arrange them in rows on the table. You can also arrange the cards so that the cards with multiplication equations are on the left side of the table and the cards with arrays are on the right side of the table.

2. The first student turns over two cards and looks to see if they are a match. If you arranged the cards with the multiplication equations on the left and the arrays on the right, the student should turn over one card from each pile.

3. If the two cards are a match, the student answers the multiplication problem and keeps the cards. If the cards are not a match, turn them back over. Cards are a match if the number of rows and columns in the array mirror the factors in the multiplication problem. For example: matches ⣿ because 2 x 3 = 2 rows and 3 columns

4. The remaining students take turns and repeat steps 2 - 3.

5. The student who collected the greatest number of cards at the end of the game wins!

DIFFERENTIATION

- Use the Set A with beginning students and Set B with advanced students.
- To help beginning students, have students write the number of rows and columns on each array card. For example:

2 x 2

1 x 4

CARD SET A

4 x 4

1 x 8

A

A

A

A

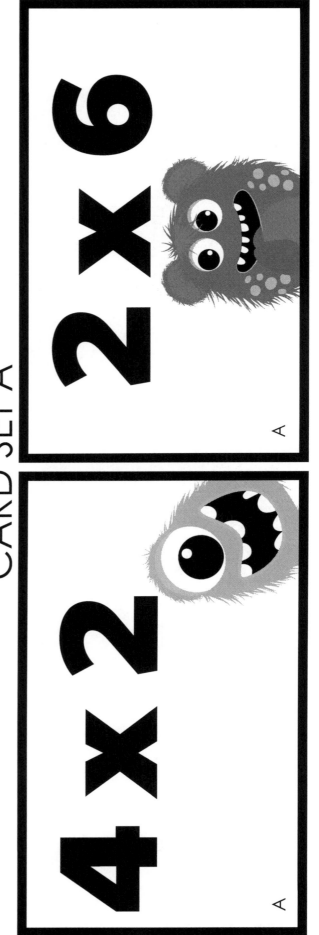

7 x 1

2 x 6

A

A

CARD SET A

2 x 3

4 x 2

A

A

7 x 2

5 x 5

CARD SET A

5 x 3

2 x 5

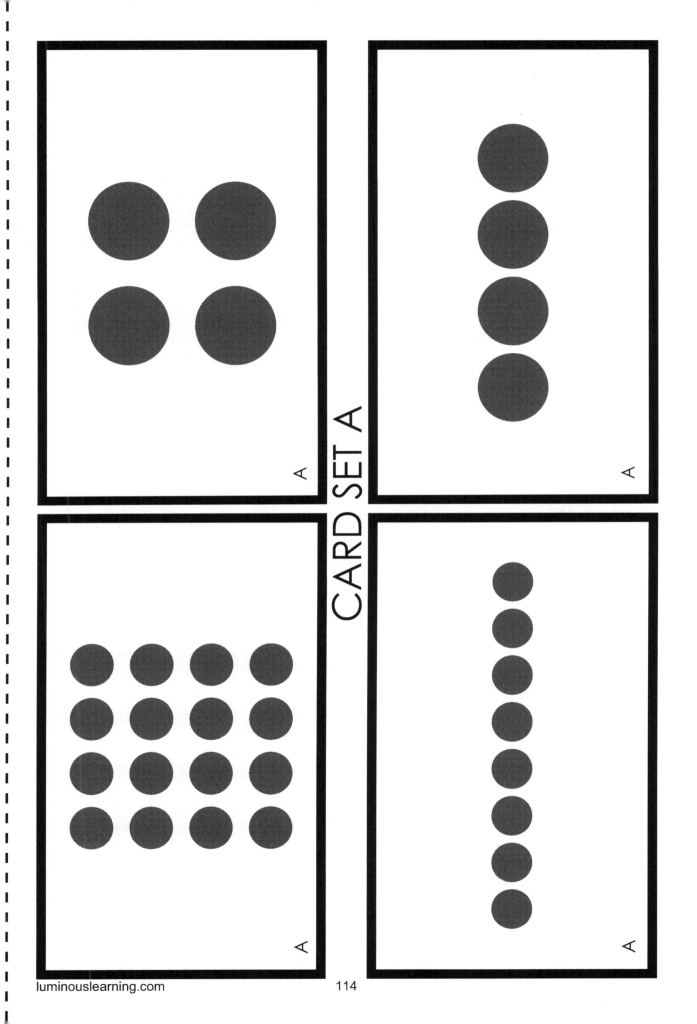

CARD SET A

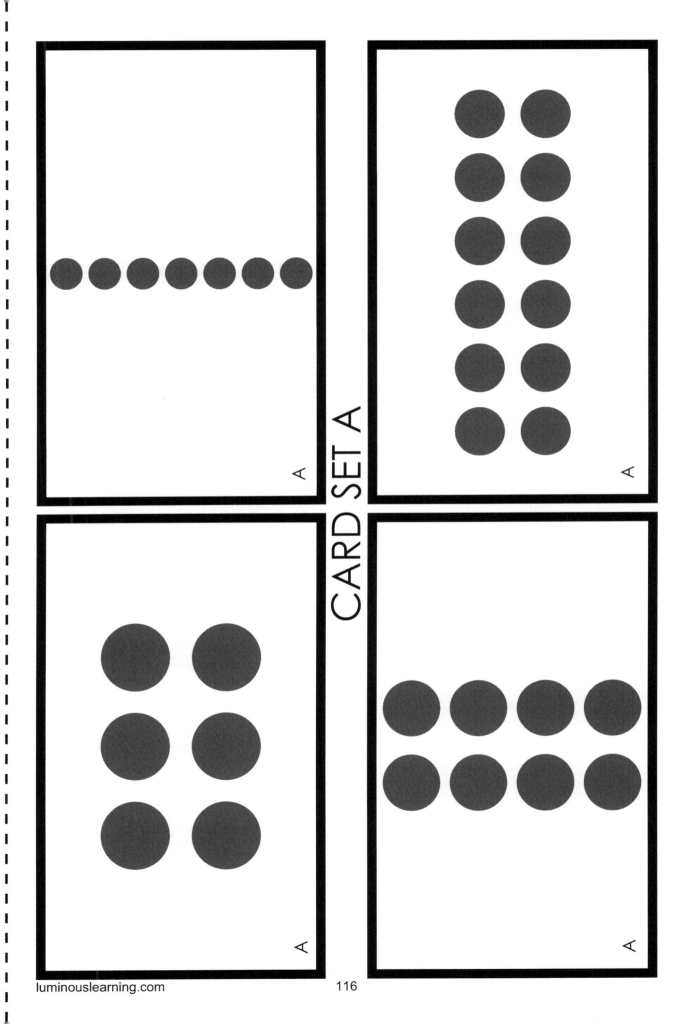

CARD SET A

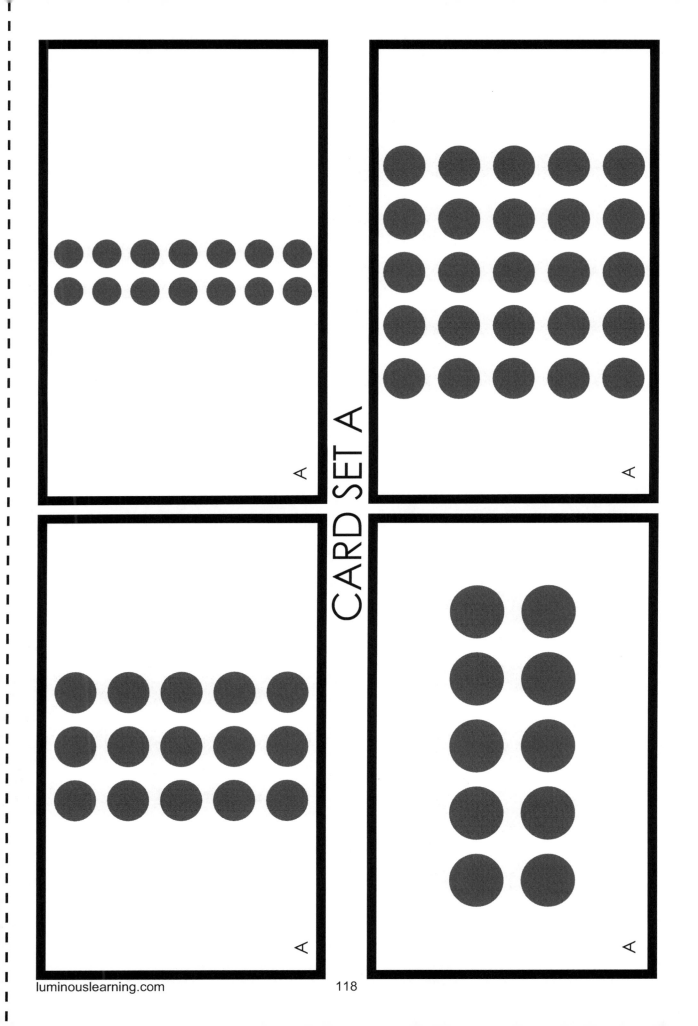

4 x 3

4

B

3 x 7

3

B

CARD SET B

3 x 6

B

3 x 8

3

B

4 x 7
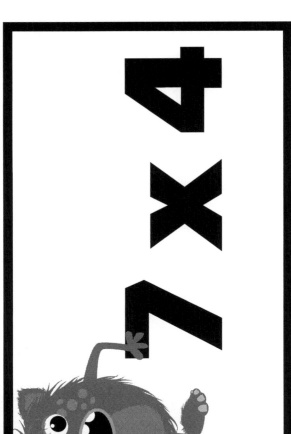

7 x 4

4 x 7

6 x 4
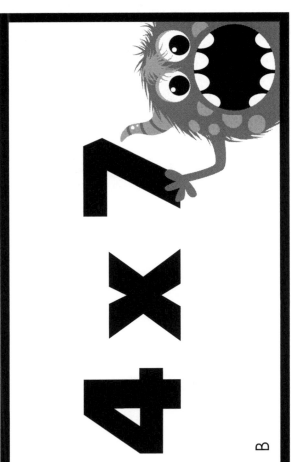

8 x 4

CARD SET B

B

B

B

B

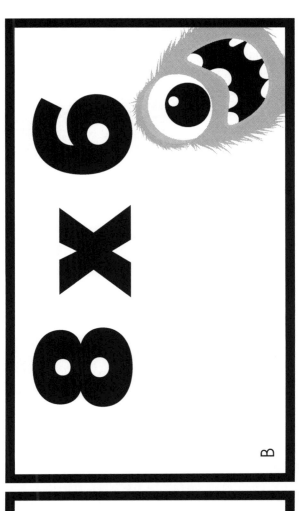

8 x 6

B

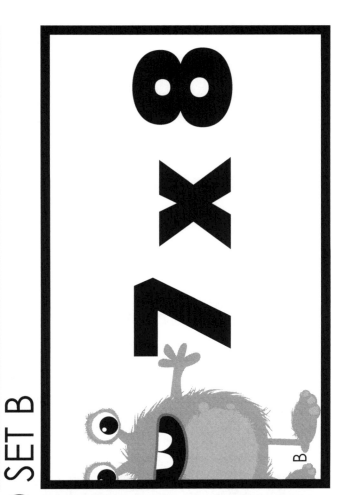

8 x 7

CARD SET B

B

8 x 5

B

7 x 7

B

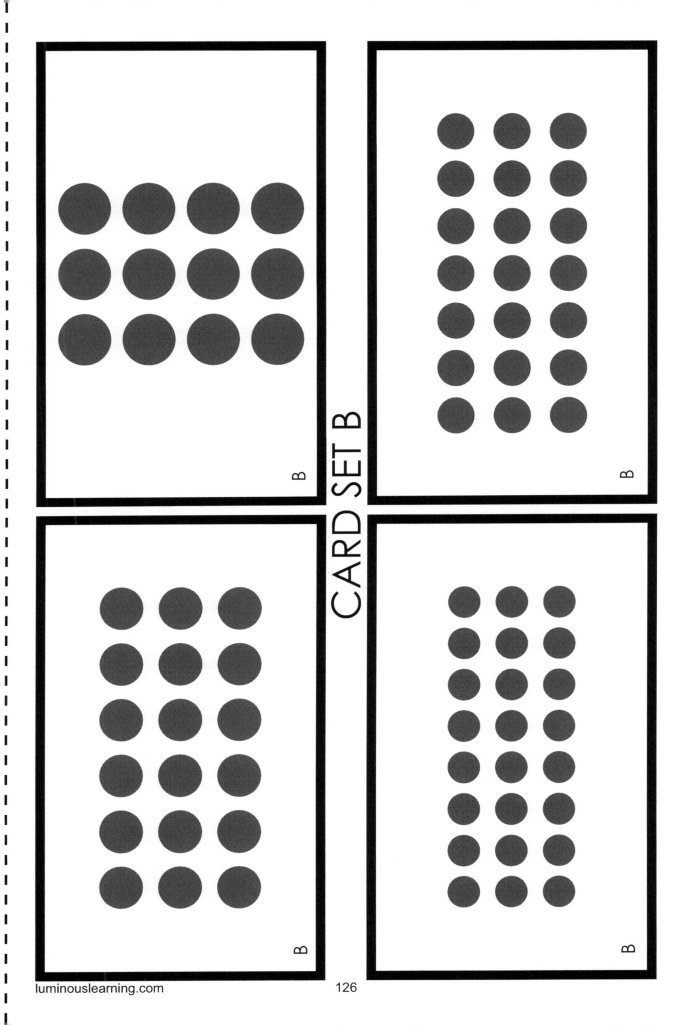

CARD SET B

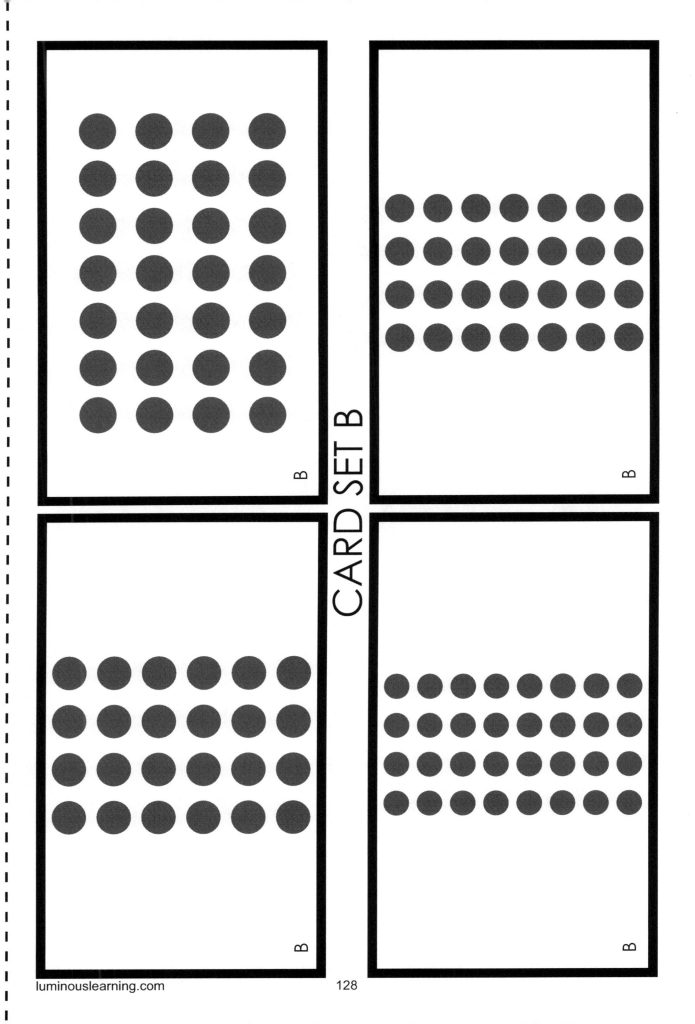

CARD SET B

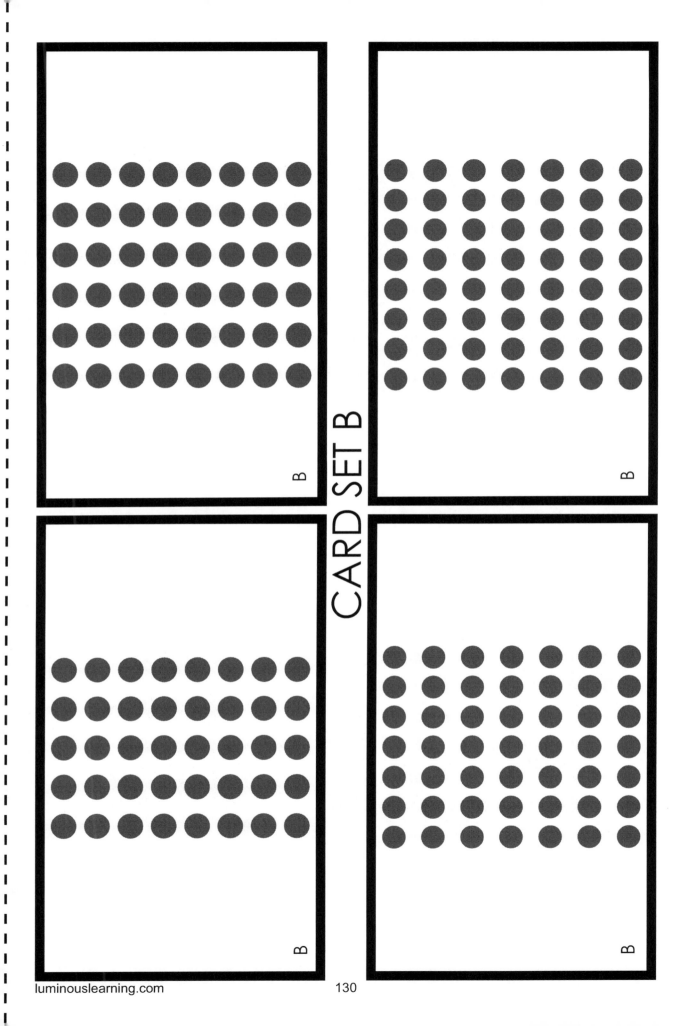

CARD SET B

Dominoes Multiplication

PLAYERS

2 - 4 students

MATERIALS

- Set of Dominoes tiles. If you don't have dominoes, you can cut out the dominoes cards in this book.
- Dominoes Multiplication recording sheet (one per student)
- Pencil

$$\underline{\quad 6 \quad} \times \underline{\quad 6 \quad} = \underline{\quad 36 \quad}$$

OBJECTIVE

Students turn over dominoes and multiply the number on either side of the domino. After solving 6 multiplication equations, students add up their products. The student with the largest sum of products wins the round!

DIRECTIONS

1. Shuffle the dominoes and lay them face down on the table.
2. Each student selects 6 dominoes. Students place each domino tile face-up on one of the gray boxes on the "Dominoes Multiplication" recording sheet. All six gray boxes should be filled with dominoes.
3. Students count the number of dots on each side of the domino tile and turn those numbers into a multiplication equation. For example, Student A has a domino with 6 dots on the left side and 6 dots on the right side. Student A writes "6 x 6" in the blanks below the domino tile.
4. Students solve each of their multiplication equations and write the products in the blanks.
5. After they are done solving all six multiplication equations, each student adds to find the sum of all six products. The student with the highest sum of their products wins the round!
6. Students can start again from #1 with a new set of recording sheets.

DIFFERENTIATION

- To make this activity easier, remove the dominoes with the more difficult problems and only have students play with the simpler problems.
- Make scratch paper or manipulatives available for those students who need to model a multiplication problem using physical materials or drawings.
- Students who need more support can partner up and play as a team. Students who need less support can play individually.

Name: _____   Date: _____

Dominoes Multiplication
Recording Sheet

_____ X _____ = _____

_____ X _____ = _____

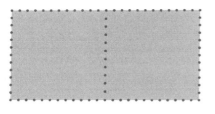

_____ X _____ = _____

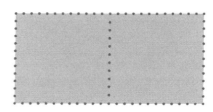

_____ X _____ = _____

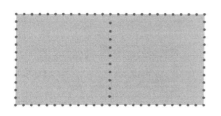

_____ X _____ = _____

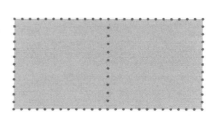

_____ X _____ = _____

Dominoes

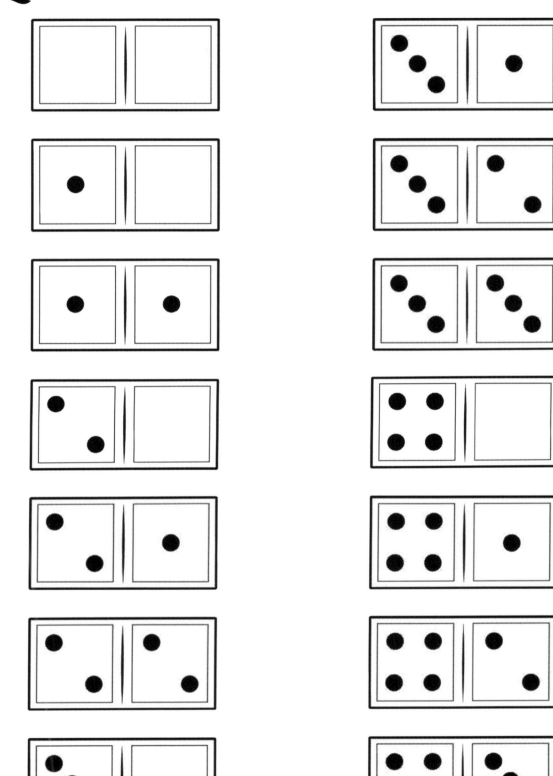

Dominoes

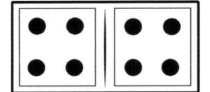

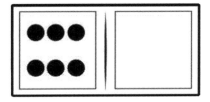

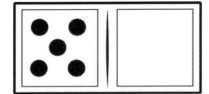

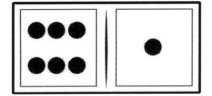

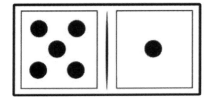

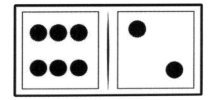

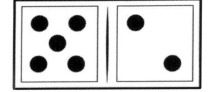

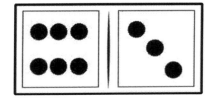

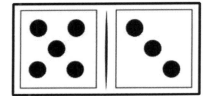

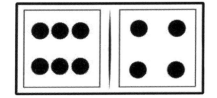

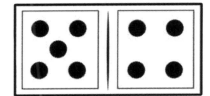

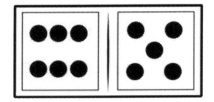

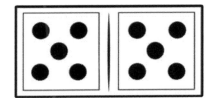

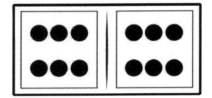

Robo-Math

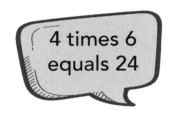

4 times 6
equals 24

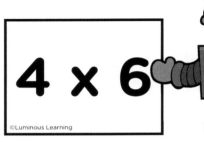

4 x 6

©Luminous Learning

PLAYERS

2 - 4 students

MATERIALS

- Robo-Math gameboard. Cut out or photocopy on thick card stock. Tape or glue both sides of the gameboard together.
- One set of Robo-Math cards. Cut out each card or photocopy on thick card stock.
- Counters or game pieces
- Die

OBJECTIVE

Students take turns answering the multiplication problem on each card. Then they roll the die to see how many spaces to move around the gameboard. The first player to reach the finish line wins!

DIRECTIONS

1. Shuffle the Robo-Math cards and place face-down in a pile. Have students place their game pieces on START.
2. Students roll the die to see who goes first. The student who rolls the highest number goes first and they continue to take turns in a clockwise direction.
3. The first student turns over the top card in the deck. The student reads the multiplication equation aloud and solves it before they can roll the die. For example, Student A turns over a card and reads, "4 times 6 equals 24."
4. The student rolls the die and moves their game piece according to the number they rolled. For example, if Student A rolls a 3, they will move their game piece ahead 3 squares.
5. The next student takes a turn and turns over the next card in the deck. Students continue to take turns solving the multiplication equations on each card and rolling to die to move their game pieces ahead. The first student to reach FINISH wins!

DIFFERENTIATION

- Make scratch paper or manipulatives available for those students who need to model a multiplication problem using physical materials or drawings.
- Students who need more support can partner up and play as a team. Students who need less support can play individually.

START

Move ahead 2 spaces

Move back 1 space

Move back 3 spaces

Take an extra turn

Robo-Math Cards

2 x 1

©Luminous Learning

2 x 2

©Luminous Learning

2 x 3

©Luminous Learning

2 x 4

©Luminous Learning

Robo-Math Cards

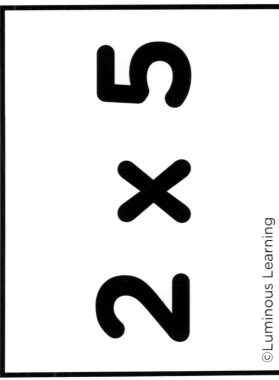

2 × 5

©Luminous Learning

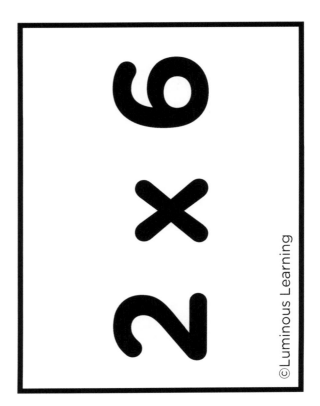

2 × 6

©Luminous Learning

2 × 7

©Luminous Learning

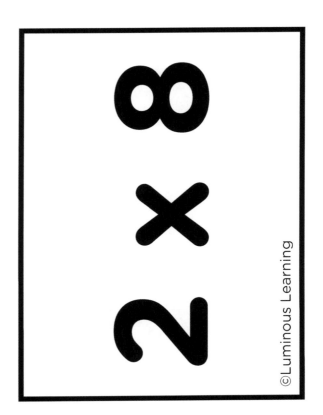

2 × 8

©Luminous Learning

Robo-Math Cards

3 × 1
3

©Luminous Learning

3 × 2
3

©Luminous Learning

3 × 3
3

©Luminous Learning

3 × 4
3

©Luminous Learning

Robo-Math Cards

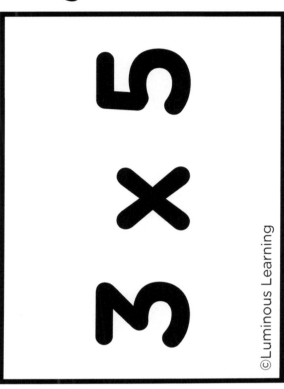

3 × 5

©Luminous Learning

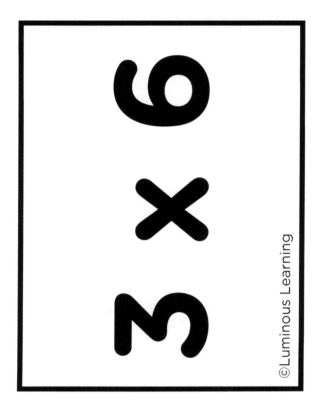

3 × 6

©Luminous Learning

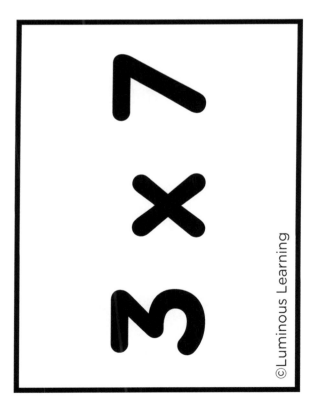

3 × 7

©Luminous Learning

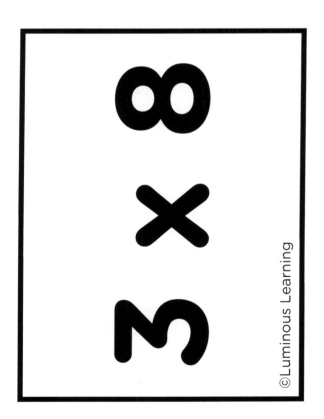

3 × 8

©Luminous Learning

Robo-Math Cards

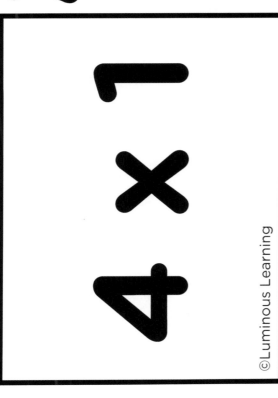

4 × 1

©Luminous Learning

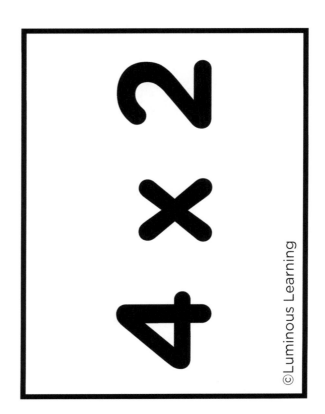

4 × 2

©Luminous Learning

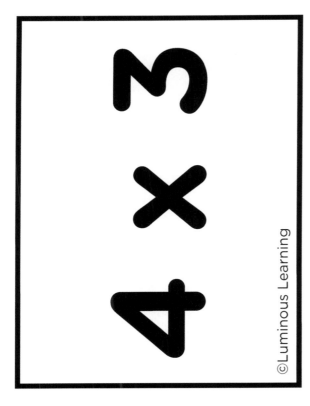

4 × 3

©Luminous Learning

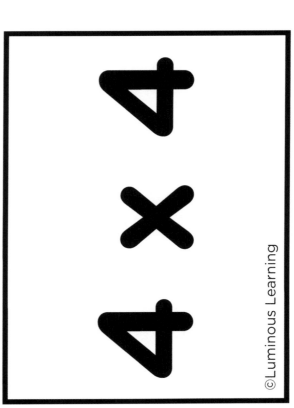

4 × 4

©Luminous Learning

Robo-Math Cards

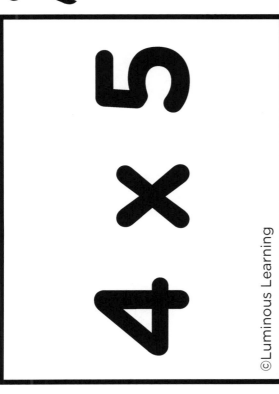

4 x 5

©Luminous Learning

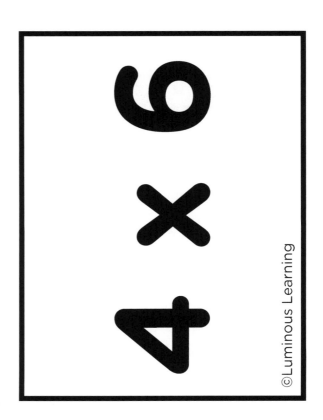

4 x 6

©Luminous Learning

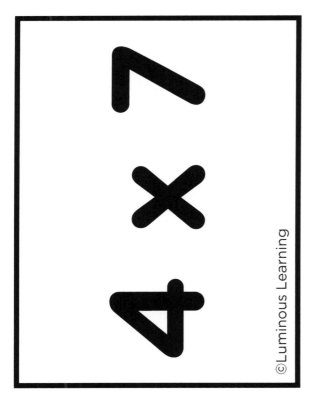

4 x 7

©Luminous Learning

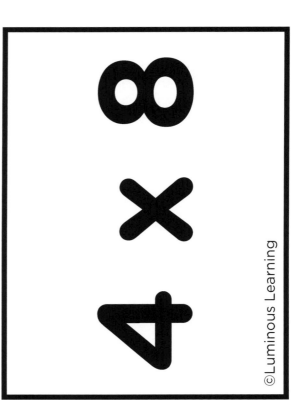

4 x 8

©Luminous Learning

Robo-Math Cards

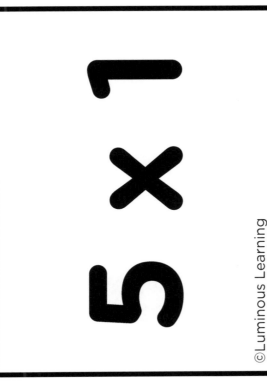

5 x 1

©Luminous Learning

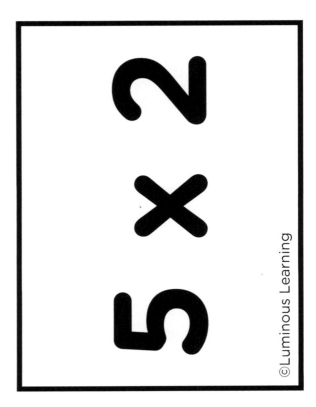

5 x 2

©Luminous Learning

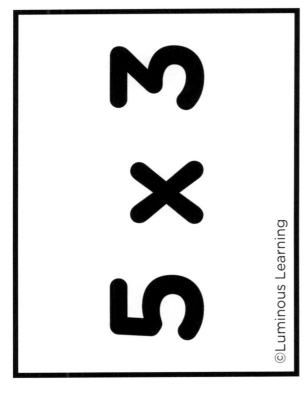

5 x 3

©Luminous Learning

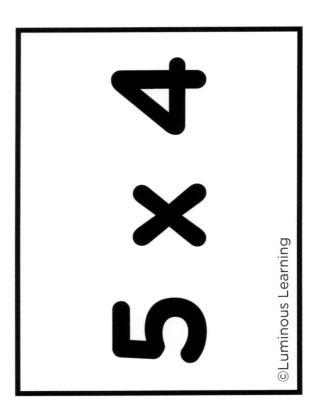

5 x 4

©Luminous Learning

Robo-Math Cards

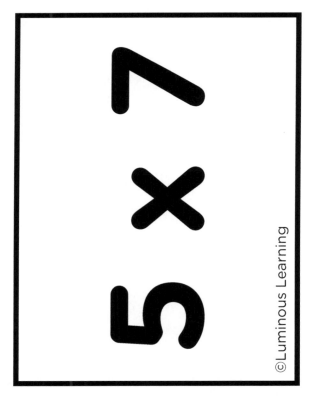

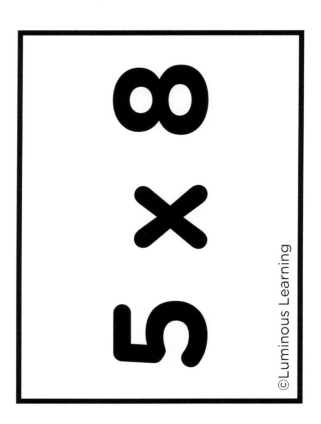

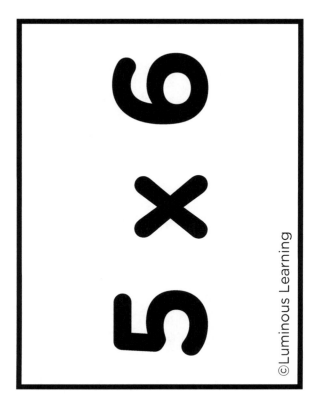

5 x 5
©Luminous Learning

5 x 6
©Luminous Learning

5 x 7
©Luminous Learning

5 x 8
©Luminous Learning

Robo-Math Cards

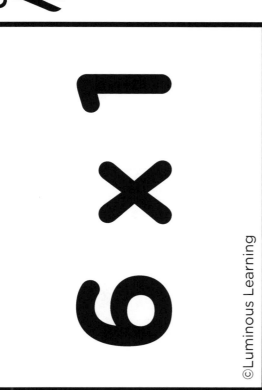

6 x 1

©Luminous Learning

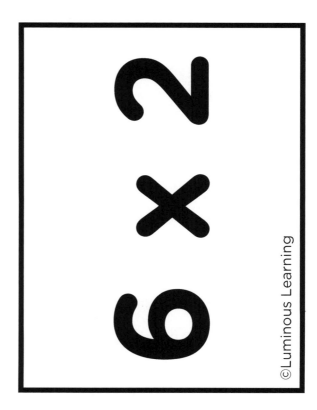

6 x 2

©Luminous Learning

6 x 3

©Luminous Learning

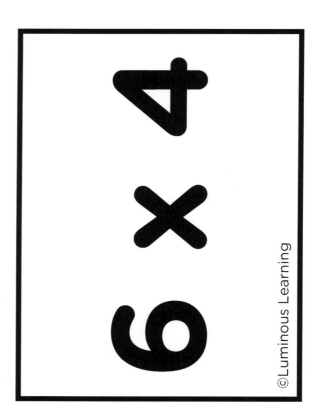

6 x 4

©Luminous Learning

Robo-Math Cards

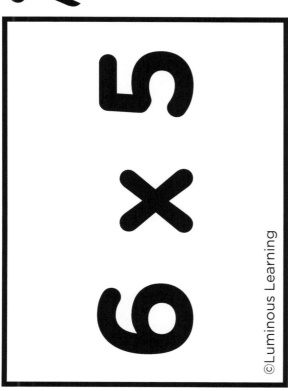

6 x 5

©Luminous Learning

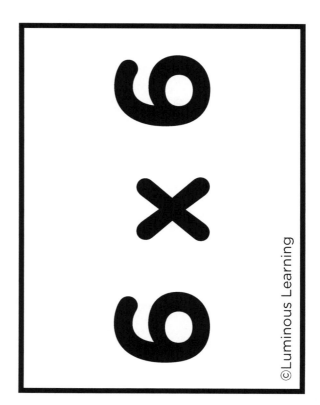

6 x 6

©Luminous Learning

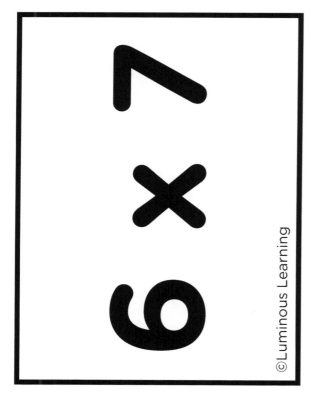

6 x 7

©Luminous Learning

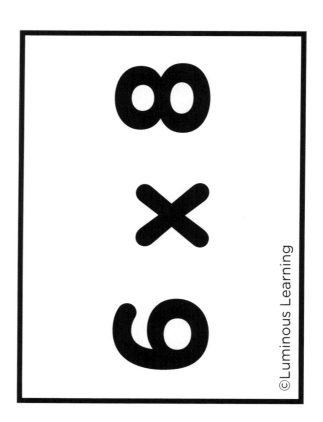

6 x 8

©Luminous Learning

Robo-Math Cards

7 x 1

©Luminous Learning

7 x 2

©Luminous Learning

7 x 3

©Luminous Learning

7 x 4

©Luminous Learning

Robo-Math Cards

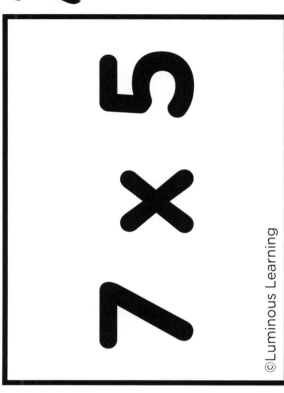

7 x 5

©Luminous Learning

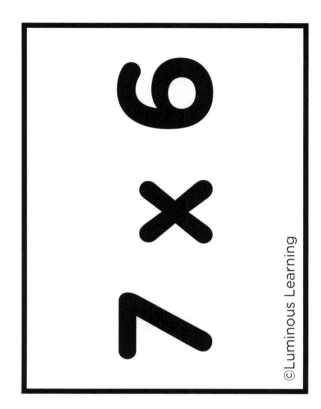

7 x 6

©Luminous Learning

7 x 7

©Luminous Learning

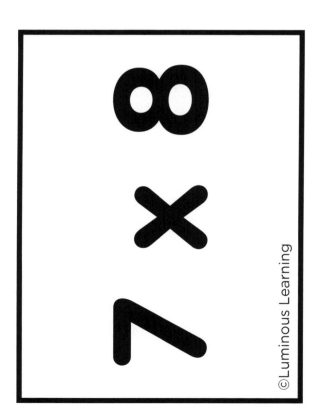

7 x 8

©Luminous Learning

Robo-Math Cards

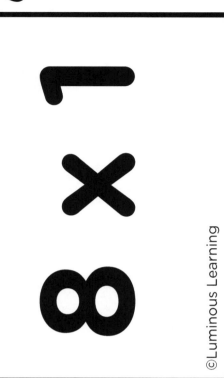

8 x 1

©Luminous Learning

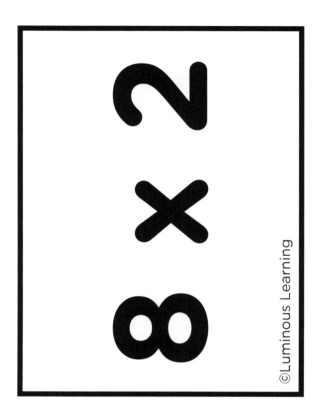

8 x 2

©Luminous Learning

8 x 3

©Luminous Learning

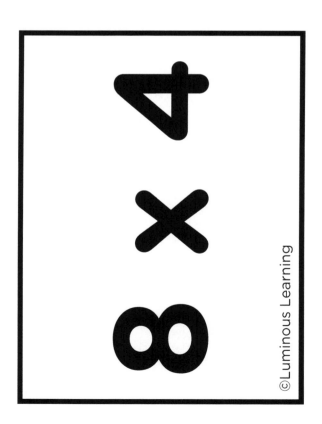

8 x 4

©Luminous Learning

Robo-Math Cards

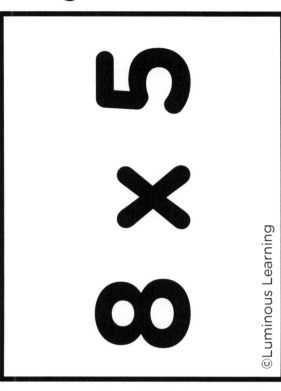

8 x 5

©Luminous Learning

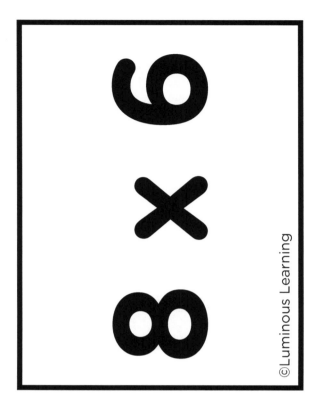

8 x 6

©Luminous Learning

8 x 7

©Luminous Learning

8 x 8

©Luminous Learning

Card Showdown!

PLAYERS

2 - 4 students

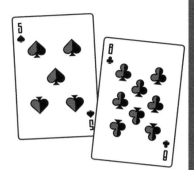

MATERIALS

- Deck of playing cards

  *You can make the Ace a "1" and pull out the Jack, Queen, and King so that you are only playing with the Ace and cards 2 through 10.

OBJECTIVE

To collect the most cards.

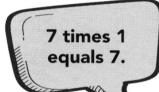

DIRECTIONS

1. Shuffle all the cards in the deck and turn the deck upside down.
2. Student 1 starts by drawing two cards from the top of the deck.
3. Next, student 2 draws two cards from the top of the deck.
4. Each student turns over their cards at the same time. Each card represents a factor in a multiplication equation. For example, if a student draws a 6 and a 2, the multiplication equation is 6 times 2. Students take turns reading their multiplication equations and the product aloud. For example, "6 times 2 equals 12."
5. The student with the highest product wins the round and takes all 4 cards. If there is a tie, each student takes another two cards and multiplies them. The student with the highest product wins all 8 cards from the tie round.
6. If you play with more than 2 students, use two decks of cards.
7. The objective of the game is to have the greatest number of cards by the end of the game. When there are no more cards left in the draw pile, students should count all their cards. The student with the most cards is the winner!

DIFFERENTIATION

- To make this activity easier, pull out the larger numbers from the deck and have students play using only smaller factors (for example, only factors 1 through 5).
- To make this activity more challenging, use all the cards, including the larger numbers (for example, factors 1 through 10).

Made in the USA
Columbia, SC
30 June 2020